DIMENSIONS OF SCHEDULED CASTE DEVELOPMENT IN INDIA
PROBLEMS AND PROSPECTS

Dimensions of Scheduled Caste Development in India

PROBLEMS AND PROSPECTS

Edited by
R.S. Tripathi and P.D. Tiwari

UPPAL PUBLISHING HOUSE
NEW DELHI—110002

UPPAL PUBLISHING HOUSE
3, Ansari Road, Daryaganj, New Delhi-110002

First Edition 1991
ISBN 81-85024-99-5

Printed in India
Published by B.S. Uppal, Uppal Publishing House
3, Ansari Road, Daryaganj, New Delhi-110002
Printed at Sainion Printary, Delhi - 11 00 32.

Preface

The people of Scheduled Castes are the most important section of Indian society, though they secure the lowest rank in Hindu castes hierarchy. In the remote past, they as 'Sudras' served the people of upper castes. They lived and worked under the influence of upper castes. They had their no voice and choice in equal attainment of human rights. They had been subjected to acute social injustice. In all, they sufferred in many ways for no fault of theirs. This long lasting situation entrapped the unfortunate Scheduled Castes people in the whirl of subjugation and explaitation. No significant changes came in their life during the long course of time.

As like in the part, the Scheduled Castes people wherever they live, are severly faced with various social, economic and political handicaps throughout the country. They are everywhere recognised as inferior to other communities. Further stratifiction is there within themselves. Economically they are poorest among the poors. Most of them are working as agricultural labourers. They are, thus, engaged in menial jobs which further aggrevate their social and ritual status. They are living a traditional social life which is not befitting to the tune of modern civilization. Social rank coupled with economic depression has led them to live a miserable life.

According to census of 1981, population of Scheduled Castes constitutes 15.75 of total population of India and as many as 84% of total population lives in rural areas. Quite obviously, agriculture is the main source of their livelihood.

Very recently, government has allocated some pieces of land to landless families in the form of 'Patta' but very few of them have acquired full possession over the land on account of various reasons. The land, if one has, does not meet their bare needs. Naturally, labouring comes in the fate of their life for survival. Scheduled Castes labourers do not get minimum wages in many parts of the country. They still work under old 'Jajmani System.' They live an indebted life and sometimes in long run, they become bonded labourer. According to an estimate, two thirds of bonded labourers are Scheduled Castes. Their housing conditions are very much deplorable. Diray surroundings, congested living, social tension, child beating querreling etc., are the common characteristics of their habitat.

Our government has made many efforts for their all round development. Constitutional provisions have been made from time to time to safeguard their interests. Policy of 'Protective Discrimination' towards weaker sections was adopted. A good policy was formulated to include the members of backward classes in government services, certain posts have been made reserved. In administration, right from village panchayat to Parliament, there is representation of Scheduled Castes. Towards social equality, constitution prohibits discrimination on the ground of castes, creed, race, language, place of birth or any other. Practice of untouchability has been abolished. A good number of schemes have been launched to provide them occupational mobility and economic strength. So far as education is concerned, reservation facilities in admissions of various institutions of higher studies, provision of scholarship facilities to the students, special coaching classes for competative examinations are some of measures undertaken for educational upliftment of the Scheduled Castes. Exercise of these provision has not brought satisfactory results. One of the aims of welfare state is to bring a state of balanced development in every walk of the society but glaring inequalities are very much noticed within the society not only in social hierarchy but also in economic situation. The Scheduled Castes occupy the rank which was ascribed to them in the past. They are still very much poor and untouchable. Due to poverty striken society, they could not avail full benefits of the provisions. Even after 43 years of Independence, economic distress and social injustice continue to remain a formidable problem to be tackled. During the plan-period, massine expenditure has been made to uplift their social and economic status, Main aim of the 7th plan was to continue the emphasis made towards the social and economic upliftment of Scheduled Castes. According to the 7th plan document, "much still remains to be done towards organisational improvements." Approach to the 8th plan also considered the efforts made heretofore as inadequate. Approach paper to the 8th plan accepts that Scheduled Castes are one of the most adversely affected section of the society. The paper asserts that a strategy for development of Scheduled Castes should lead to a programme that effectively liberates them from their age-old disabilities.

The problems faced with the Scheduled Castes can not be tackled untill diagnostic studies are undertaken. The researches covering all the significant aspects are very much required to unfold the basic characteristics of the glaring problems. With this aim in mind, an attempt has been made to collected research contributions devoted to the Scheduled Castes. It is hoped that the thoughts contained in this volume will be of much help for the personnel concerned with the development of Scheduled Castes.

14th. April, 1991

Prof. R.S. TRIPATHI
Atarra P.G. College, Atarra
Dist. Banda, U.P.
Dr. P.D. TIWARI
Reader
Dr. H.S. Gaur University
Sagar (M.P.)

Dt. April 2, 1991

Dr. R.P. TIWARI
Reader
Dr. H.S. Gour University
Sagar (M.P.)

Contents

Contributors

1. Impact of Caste on Primary Occupations in India
Dr. Noor Mohammad
Associate Professor of Geography
Department of Geography
Delhi School of Economics
University of Delhi
Delhi - 110007

2. Sex Disparity in Scheduled Caste Literacy in Maharashtra: A Case of Selected Villages
Dr. Krishan Chand Ramotra
Lecturer in Geography
Department of Geography
Shivaji University, Kolhapur - 416004

3. Literary of Scheduled Castes in Bundelkhand Region, Utter Pradesh : A Spatial Analysis
Dr. R.K. Shukla
Senior lecturer in Geography
Department of Geography
Atarra P.G. College, Atarra
Dist. Banda, Uttar Paradesh
Dr. Chunna Singh
Head of the Department
Department of Geography
F.S.L. Govt. Degree College
Jalaun, Uttar Pradesh

4. Areal Profiles of Scheduled Castes Concentration in the Economic Sectors of Uttar Pradesh
Dr. Surendra Singh
Department of Geography
North-Eastern Hill University, Shillong - 793014

5. Women's Age at Marriage Among Scheduled Castes and its Implications : Theoritical and Empirical Explorations
Dr. S.B. Singh Parmar
Department of Sociology
Atarra P.G. College, Atarra
Dist. Banda, Uttar Pradesh

6. Chaning the Status of the Scheduled Castes
Dr. R.L. Maurya
Lecturer in Sociology
Department of Sociology
Government P.G. College, Pithoragarh

7. Nutrition Problems and Diseases Caused by Malnutrition Among Scheduled Castes
Dr. R.P. Tiwari
Asst. Professor of Geography
Goverment P.G. College
Tikamgarh (M.P.)
Dr. R.S. Tripathi
Lecturer in Geogaphy
Atarra P.G. College, Atarra
Dist. Banda, Uttar Pradesh

8. On the Problems of Schduled Castes Observations of Harijan Elites
Dr. R.G. Dwivedi
Department of Geography
Atarra P.G. College, Atarra
Dist. Banda, Uttar Pradesh

9. Harijans : Their Conversion and Problem
Prof. A. Satyanarayana Moorthy
Proffessor in Sociology

ONE

Impact of Caste on Primary Occupations in India

A GEOGRAPHICAL ANALYSIS

Dr. Noor Mohammad

Conceptual Framework

Caste and primary occupations are so closely linked to each other that they are quite often taken as synonyms. In the past every caste had an occupation of its own which used to be hereditary and to abondon it in search of others was considered to be sinful. But with the passage of time both have changed considerably. The purity of caste exists only in religious books. Inter-caste and inter-religion marriages and the cross breeds of their off-springs have resulted into innumerable castes. Similarly the occupational ramification was so rapid and diverse that several thousand of occupations are being adopted by inhabitants of the world. In fact during the twentieth century considerable technological changes have taken place leading to the improvement of overall economic condition of the people on the one hand and the socio-political upliftment of the masses on the other. Revolution has taken place in industrial and agricultural sector and the transport technoloy does not lag behind. The population has increased manyfold and the dietry habit of the people is changing fast. In dairy, poultry and piggeries several new breeds and birds are added which make them more profitable.

However, under such an overall caste-occupation dynamism, caste-occupation relationship at micro scale still exits. The degree of relationship depends, by and large, on level of technological development and modernisation. In backward and rural areas the primary occupations are still associated with certain castes. Since it is their hereditary occupation, they know all its techniques, methods, ins and out leading to higher production. We should, therefore, encourage the development of primary occupation according to the caste which have it on hereditary ground and the micro level planning should be done on this basis. Therefore, it is essential to study caste-occupation relationship for a rational and meaningful planning for the overall development of a region. For this purpose the State of Uttar Pradesh has been taken in the present study as it was not possible to collect the primary data for the entire country.

The Geographical Profile of the Region

The State of Utter Pradesh, situated in the northern part of India between 23° 52′-31° 28′ N. Lat. and 77 04-84 38 E. Long., covers an area of 294,362 square kilometres. It had 48 districts in 1931 which have now been split into 56 districts (Fig. 1). Lying in the Ganga plain, the entire state, with few exceptions, is a vast homogeneous plain mainly drained by the rivers Ganga, Yamuna, Gomati and Ghaghara. The state enjoys sub-humid climate with three well marked seasons : summer, rainy and winter. The soil is fertile allivium deposited by the river channels. It has a predominantly agrarian structure. Agriculture engage roughly 80 per cent of the total population directly or indirectly, is the main occupation of the people and it provides more than 50 per cent of state income. The state is not favourably endowed with mineral resources and its industrial base is also comparatively poor. It has a fairly good network of transport and communication, although there are a lot of variations in it. Uttar Pradesh is one of the densely populated states of the country and has a very complex population structure. It is more so in case of caste composition of population. More than hundred castes are found here but the major ones are Brahmin, Rajput, Jat, Shaikh, Kurmi, Scheduled caste, Kori etc. Since the state is at comparatively low web of the level of technological advancement, the association between caste and primary occupation is more glaring and strong but it has not been studied so far.

Overview of Literature

The caste and its various parameters have been thoroughly studied at international, national and regional levels in spatio-temporal perspectives. The caste system, its nature, structure has also been elaborately studied by sociologists, anthropologists and ethnographers. The caste, class and power have been one of the major themes of study of sociologists. Similary various primary, secondary and tertiary occupations have also been a major theme of study for the geographers in particular, and economists and historians in general. The occupational structure of population has also been a piont of study for geographers, demographers, economists, sociologists, and historians all over the world (Berry, et. al, 1978) Enumeration of occupation has been one of the major themes of the census organisations in almost all countries of the world.

Thus there are plenty of documents and literature on these two components viz., caste and occupation. But there is a derth of studies literature dealing with these two components together giving their inter and intra-relationships. Risley's (1915) study of caste composition and some of the major occupations at Indian census of 1901, is the poineer work done on the national scale and under government aegis. But even his study is partially successful. Sociologists and anthropologists, although mainly concerned with the study of caste, class and power, have done some study in this respect from their own points of view (Omvetd, 1980). For example, in 1945 Gadgil in his first report of the Poona survey, has published his scheme of occupational categories based on their nature and status. His study of principal weaving castes Maharashtra and the changing natue of their occupation, is one of the basic works of the caste-occupation relationship. Ghaurye (1961) has written a voluminous book on "*Caste, Class, and Occupation*" which sounds to be reasonably dealing with caste-occupation relationship. But it gives more specific treatment to caste and its correlates with a general chapter on caste and occupation. In this chapter too, a review of various studies dealing with occupation and occupational structure has been given with specific mention of few studies which deal with caste and occupation at micro or regional levels.

The geographers did study the primary occupations specially crop farming, dairy farming, vegetable farming etc., but they were busy in analysing the spatial distribution of agricuture with respest to physio-economic conditions (Singh. 1970, Mohammad, 1978, Symon, 1978), and the institutional bases of agriculture, especially caste, have not been studied in proper perspectives. The studies which are available, are sketchy and too general in this respect (Buchanan, 1969, Symon, 1978, Mohammad, 1981, and Singh, 1985). Thus in geographical literature the study of caste and primary occupation is almost non-existant as far as the author knows. The author has given Field-Survey Projects on Impact of Caste on Primary Occupations to his M.A. final year students. The Survey had been conducted in different villages located in the Union Territory of Delhi, and it gives different kind of association between caste and primary occupation which has prompted the author to conduct a thorough study to assess the relationship between caste and primary occupations.

Data Source and Methodology

The study is essentially based on primary data collected from 1033 respondents of different castes chosen from 35 sample villages which have been taken from each caste-combination regions worked out on Doi's method using 1931 data for caste, as it is the only secondary data available on caste. These respondents have been interviewed according to a well structured questionnaire which besides containing a number of quarries, focuses on six primary occupations viz., crop farming, vegetable farming, dairy farming, poultry farming, fish farming, and piggeries. Besides these, there are other occupations being followed by the people due to the variety of reasons, which have been broadlyput into service, labour and other occupations. These occupations have also been discussed along with the primary occupations. The data thus collect have been processed and analysed in order to examine and explain the association between the caste and the selected occupations. A detailed account of each selected caste and its occupation is given below.

Brahmins and their Primary Occupations

Brahmin—the levile class of Hindu caste system, who were once upon a time considered as priests, worshippers, composer or reciter of hymns, have varied occupations (Crooke, 1974). There are 204 total Brahmin respondents, out of which 162 or about 80 per cent have crop farming as their first occupation. The remaining 20 per cent have dairy farming, vegetable farming, service, labour and other occupations. The heavy dependence of Brahmins on crop farming is due to three reasons: firstly, their priestly occupation which was, of course, very remunerative in the past, has become almost obsolete; secondly, they have land which they have got, perhaps, from landlords and jagirdars as a result of performing religious, social and cultural rituals; and thirdly, the younger generation of Brahmins does not want to go by their hereditary occupation. Therefore, firstly they started crop farming by engaging people lower castes as labourers, as ploughing by Brahmins was declared by themselves as against religion. But now with changed socio-economic conditions and non-availability of

TABLE I

Nmmber of Respondents from each Caste

Sl. No.	*Castes*	*No. of Respondents*	*% age of total*
1.	Brahmin	204	19.75
2.	Rajput	123	11.91
3.	Scheduled castes	235	22.85
4.	Jat	38	3.68
5.	Nomads	14	1.36
6.	Shaikh	85	8.04
7.	Kurmi	49	4.75
8.	Ahir	139	13.47
9.	Pasi	69	6.69
10.	Kachhi	14	1.36
11.	Lodhi	17	1.68
12.	Kori	18	1.75
13.	Other castes	28	2.71
	Total	1033	100.00

agricultural labourers, they have started ploughing the land themselves. There are 27 Brahmins or 18.12 per cent of the total 149 Brahmins who have crop farming as their second occupation, while only 4 Brahmins have crop farming as their third occupation. And as such, if Brahmins with crop farming as their first, second and third occupation, are put together, they account about 94 per cent of the total respondents. Except in poultry farming and piggeries, Brahmins have all the selected occupations. A comparative study of crop production and crop productivity of different castes indicates that Brahmin respondents are in a better position as compared to other castes. The production of wheat, rice and sugarcane among Brahmin respondents is much higher.

Vegetable farming is the other occupation engaging more than one-third of the total Brahmin respondents. About 4 per cent have vegetable farming as first occupation, while 17 per cent have it as their second occupation, although they account 24 per cent of Brahmins of this group. About 17 per cent of total Brahmin respondents or 34 per cent of Brahmins with vegetable farming as their occupation, have vegetable farming as third occupation. The heavy concentration of Brahmins in vegetable farming is due to their dietary habits being governed by religious and socio-cultural laws, which do not permit them to be non-vegetarian. So vegetable constitute a major item in their diet. But the vegetable production is unsatisfactory among Brahmin respondents. The production of potato is, of course, higher among them.

About 32 per cent Brahmin respondents have dairy farming as their first, second and third occupation. Five Brahmins or 2.45 per cent have dairy farming as their first occupation, while 39 Brahmin respondents have it as second occupation. They account more than 26 per cent Brahmins under this group. Twenty two Brahmins or 27.84 per cent Brahmins under third occupation, have dairy farming as their third occupation. Surprisingly 4 Brahmins have fishing as third occupation. In fact dairy farming, by and large, is not their basic occupation. They practice it on subsistance basis.

More than 37 per cent Brahmins are in service either having it as first, second or third occupation. It is a main occupation

TABLE II

Brahmins and their Primary Occupations

Occupations	*First No. of Respon*	*Occupation % age*	*Second No. of Respon.*	*Occupation % age*	*Third No. of Respon*	*Occupation % age*
Crop farming	162	79.41	27	18.12	4	5.06
Dairy farming	5	2.45	39	28.17	22	27.84
Fishing	—	—	—	—	4	5.06
Vegetable farming	8	3.92	35	23.49	27	34.18
Poultry farming	—	—	—	—	—	—
Piggeries	—	—	—	—	—	—
Service	20	9.80	44	29.53	13	16.46
Labour	8	3.92	4	2.69	1	1.27
Others	1	0.50	—	—	8	10.13
Total	204	100.00	149	100.00	99	100.00

of about one-third of Brahmins, while secondary occupation of 21 per cent. About 7 per cent Brahmins are engaged in services as their third occupation. A scrutiny of questionnaire shows that Brahmins are, by and large, in white collar jobs. The poor Brahmins constituting about 6 per cent of the total, are labourers Out of which for about 4 per cent, it is a main occupation, while for 4 respondents it is second occupation. Only one respondent considers it as his third occupation. Nine Brahmins accounting more than 4 per cent of the total, have miscellaneous occupations. This analysis shows that majority of Brahmins have crop farming followed by service and dairy farming.

Rajput and their Primary Occupations

Rajputs are considered to be warrior and ruling caste, and even to-day they constitute a major segment of Indian army. But however, due to changing socio-economic conditions, they are also changing their occupations. Crop farming is their major occupation engaging about 85 per cent of the Rajput respondents (Table, III). About 78 per cent Rajputs have crop farming as their first occupation. Only one Rajputs has crop farming as his third occupation, while 20 Rajput have it as second occupation. Due to several favourable socio-economic factors, the crop productivity among Rajput respondents is also high.

Dairy farming is an other popular occupation among Rajputs engaging about 37 per cent of the total respondents. Only 5 Rajputs have it as first occnpation, while 23 as second. Seventeen Rajputs have dairy farming as their third occupation, which is about one-third of the respondents under this category. Rajputs are not the professional dairy farmers. They keep it on subsistence basis. The overall production in dairy farming among Rajput respondents is low. Vegetable farming is almost equally popular among Rajputs accounting about 30 per cent of total respondents under it. Twenty three respondents have vegetable

TABLE III

Rajputs and their Primary Occupations

Occupations	*First No. of Respon.*	*Occupation % age*	*Second No. of. Respon.*	*Occupation % age*	*Third No. of Respon*	*Occupation % age*
Crop farming	96	78.05	20	21.74	1	2.27
Dairy farming	5	4.07	23	25.00	17	38.63
Fishing	—	—	2	2.17	3	6.83
Vegetable Farming	2	1.63	23	25.00	12	27.27
Poultry Farming	—	—	—	—	1	2.27
Piggeries	—	—	—	—	—	—
Service	16	13.00	21	22.83	10	22.73
Labour	4	3.25	3	3.26	—	—
Others	—	—	—	—	—	—
Total	123	100.00	92	100.00	44	100.00

farming as their second occupation, while 12 and 2 respondents have it as second third and first occupation respectively. Rajputs grow vegetables mostly for their own consumption with few exception who sell it as well. Recently in the villages near the market centres, Rajputs have started growing potatoes on commercial scales. Except potatoes, the other vegetables gvown by Rajputs give poor results, as they do not know the technique of doing it as well as they can not devote as much time as it requires. Although Rajputs are non-vegetarian, poultry farming and piggeries are almost absent among them except one respondent who has poultry farming as third occupation. Fishing is also not popular. Only 2 and 3 respondents have it as their second and third occupation respectively. This shows that fishing, poultry and piggeries are occupations adopted by low caste people, although its products are being consumed by high caste people. About 44 per cent, Rajputs are in service and labour. The former engages 48 per cent, while the later only 6 per cent. The main occupation of 16 respondents is service, while 12 respondents have it as their second occupation. Like Brahmins, Rajputs are also in higher position with white collar jobs. The scrutiny of survey proforma indicates that they are in military, administration, and teaching. Only 4 Rajputs have labour as their first occupation, while 3 have it as second occupation. They are the poor and illiterate Rajputs.

Scheduled Castes and their Primary Occupations

Scheduled Castes are popularly known as service and labour class since early times. In spite of all developments and modernisation, they still continue to be in the same occupation. They, being the poor and down trodden, look for their livelihood all around and wherever occupation is available, they opt for it provided they are permitted to do so. Therefore, they are seen in all categories of the selected occupations. (Table-IV). The highest percentage viz. 62 per cent is in crop farming followed by piggeries. Sixty nine respondents or 29 per cent of the total have crop farming as their first occupation, while 5.2

per cent respondents have it as second occupation. There are 24 respondents having it as third occupation. The latter two categories contribute 27 and 19 per cent of total respondents in their respective groups. Although a very low percentage of Scheduled Castes have crop farming as their first, second and third occupation, their economic condition is unsatisfactory. The scrutiny of survey proforma indicates that they are marginal or very small size of farmers with limited financial resources. They have got land under the Government's policy of distribution of land among landless. These lands were either *Banjar* lands of Gram Smaj or were acquired under Land Ceiling Act. In both the cases the quality of land is poor which is quite obvious because the land was left uncultivated and entered *Banjar* (infertile land) under *Gram Samaj*, and the farmers have given their worst quality of land in ceiling. But the Scheduled Castes who were deprived of land since ages happily accepted this land, and they are putting all their human and financial resources to get much out of it. But neither they have infrastructure for the capital to built it. Therefore, the yield is very low. A time is likely to came very soon when these respondents will give up such lands and will go back to service and labour. But those respondents are doing better who have taken land from big peasants on lease basis or on share cropping basis because these lands are fertile and infrastructure is already built up there. Moreover, land owners advance credit for purchase of agricultural inputs.

Piggeries—their ancestral occupation, stands second engaging 58 per cent of Scheduled Caste respondents. Seventy two respondents. or about 53 per cent of respondents have it as their first occupation, while 56 respondents or 41 per cent have it as their second occupation. Only 9 respondents have it as third occupation. Piggeries is their main occupation and no other caste except a few does this occupation because of the religious and social taboos. By and large, it is their subsistance occupation but recently they are converting it on commercial basis.

TABLE IV

Scheduled Castes and their Primary Occupations

Occupations	*First No. of Respon*	*Occupation % age*	*Second No. of Respon*	*Occupation % age*	*Third No. of Respon*	*Occupation % age*
Crop farming	89	29.36	52	26.80	24	19.20
Dairy farming	9	3.83	10	5.15	5	4.00
Fishing	2	0.85	23	11.86	62	49.60
Vegetable farming	—	—	12	6.19	5	4.00
Poultry farming	—	—	4	2.06	8	6.40
Piggeries	72	30.64	56	28.87	9	7.20
Service	10	4.26	7	3.60	10	8.00
Labour	70	29.79	29	14 95	1	0.80
Others	3	1.27	1	0.52	1	0.80
Total	235	100.00	194	100.00	125	100.00

The Government is giving very liberally loans for piggeries, although it is highly misutilised. But those who use it properly have developed piggeries and it has become a main source of income for them. It is very susceptible to diseases but Government has established various vaterinary hospitals to take care of it.

Fishing is third primary occupation engaging 37 per cent of Scheduled Caste respondents, although there are only 2 respondents having fishing as their first occupation. In fact fishing is main occupation of *Chai*, *Kewat* etc. who are also Scheduled Caste. There are 23 respondents, constituting 10 per cent of the total having fishing as their second occupation, while 62 respondents or 26 per cent have it as their third occupation. There are several periods in a year when fishing is done on large scale. For example, in the beginning of rainy season when drains discharge their water in rivers or perennial lakes and ponds, fishes being harassed in course of fishing during summer, want to move out from those rivers and ponds through these channels, and in this process they are being caught. Moreover, this is, by and large, their breeding period, so they are in abundance. Similarly during the summer season or even from the tail end of the winter season when the small water bodies start getting dry or the amount of water reduces in bigger ones, fishes are caught in large quantity. Therefore, due to its nature fishing can not be a main source of income in land locked states but it does provide additional income to the poor Scheduled Caste respondents.

Adoption of dairy farming by Scheduled Castes is a recent phenomenon which is the gift of modernisation and socialisation. In the early times high and medium caste people could not even think of consuming the home made commodities of Scheduled Caste or any low caste. But now a days due to the development of the various service centres in the rural areas, tea stalls and sweet shops have come up like any thing which consume large quantities of milk. They purchase milk from every milk supplier irrespective of caste. Moreover, for high caste people, keeping and maintenance of dairy cattle has become a difficult task due to shortage of labour and shrinking of the pasture and grazing lands in which they use to leave their cattle free. Besides this, in the past the high caste people use to leave their cattle free in the village outskirts and no body could dare to tell anything to them against it. But now the conditions have changed and dairy farming requires large manpower to take care of it. Hence, scheduled caste, with large manpower, are venturing in this pursuit. Moreover, the Government is providing loans with heavy subsidies to poor classes for dairy farming. However, there are 10 per cent respondents engaged in dairy farming. Out of which about 4 per cent have it as their first occupation, while almost equal percentage has is as second occupation. Five respondents have dairy farming as their third occupation. Majority of the scheduled castes dairy farmers sell the raw milk to these shops or sell it to dairy caste Ahirs, who supply it for home consumption to high and medium caste people. However, the dairy farming is giving a big economic boost to Scheduled Caste. Vegetable farming again has the same religious taboos because green vegetable grown and sold by Scheduled Caste will not be purchased by high caste people. But the conditions are changing and Scheduled Castes are also venturing in this occupation. There is none among Scheduled Caste with vegetable farming as his first occupation but there are 12 and 5 respondents having it as their second and third occupation respectively. Except few vegetables, they mostly grow it for their own consumption.

Large percentage of Scheduled Caste (42.55 per cent) respondents are labourers having it as their first, second and third occupation. Labour is main occupation of about 30 per cent respondents, while about 12 per cent have it as second occupation. There is only one respondent with labour as his third occupation. Scheduled Caste work as agricultral labourers in rural areas or as labourers in construction and manufacturing in town and cities. Recently with the taking up of several projects by Government in rural areas like the construction of roads, embankments, canals, and several small scale industries, Scheduled Caste labourers have diverted their attention towards this. As a result, there is shortage of agricultural labourers which will adversely affect agriculture in coming decades, and eventually it would lead towards mechanisation. About 11 per cent of Scheduled Caste are in service also. While 10 each have it as their first and third occupation, only 7 have it as second occupation. Although the percentage of Scheduled Caste in service is reasonable, most of them are in low paid or inferior quality jobs. A very microscopic percentage is in white collar jobs. The survey schedule indicates that majority of Scheduled Castes are sweeper in urban centres or in clerical jobs.

Jats and their Primary Occupations

Jats are medium caste Hindus but occupy higher social status due to their better economic conditions and dominance in certain localities. They are sturdy and hard working. They are considered to be most efficient cultivators of India. They are slave to their farm (Russel and Lal, 1975). They have the feel of the soil and by having better agricultural infrastructure, they have high agricultural productivity. Their absorption is rigorous out of door work at all seasons, but it has had its effect on his character and physique (Crooke, 1974). Crop farming is their main and basic occupation. About 95 per cent Jat respondents have crop farming as their first occupation which speaks itself regarding favouritism of crop farming among Jats. A scrutiny of survey schedule indicates that they are, by and large, big and medium size farmers and do crop farming on commerical basis. There are only 4 respondents having crop farming as their second occupation. (Table V). Jats are very innovative and efficient farmers. Their technological knowledge and involvement is more; and they are economically better of also. Therefore, the crop production and crop productivity among Jat farmers is highest among all castes. They mainly produce wheat, jowar, bajra and sugarcane.

Dairy farming is the next important primary occupation of Jats. Ahir and Jat have close relationship, and in certain areas they are synonyms. However, only 2 respondents who did not have crop farming as their first occupation, have dairy farming as their first occupation, while 14 Jats contributing about 54 per cent of respondents under this category, have dairy farming as their second occupation. They do this occupation on commercial and subsistence basis. Majority of them sell raw milk in the villages or in the neighbouring market centres. Jat respondents are semi-professional in dairy farming. They keep better quality dairy cattle and overall dairy product among Jat respondents is high.

Vegetable farming is also popular among Jats but mostly it is done on subsistence basis. Generally they devote a small portion of their land to vegetable farming. A microsocopic percentage of Jats sell vegetables either themselves or through middleman. But recently potato cultivation with high yielding varieties has become more remunerative. It is more so as compared to wheat which requires higher inputs on one hand and Government fixed price is very low on the other. Therefore, Jat cultivators have diverted their attention towards this. They have started devoting large areas under potato cultivation, and they sell it on commercial basis. But except potatoes, the production of other vegetables among Jats is low.

None of the Jat respondents are in poultry farming and piggeries but about 19 per cent of them are engaged in service, labour and other occupations. The majority of their percentage is in service. The detailed scrutiny of the survey schedules indicates that they are in white collar jobs such as in military, teaching and administration. There is a single Jat respondent who has labour as his second occupation.

TABLE V

Jats and their Primary Occupations

Occupations	First No. of Respon	Occupation % age	Second No. of Respon	Occupation % age	Third No. of Respon	Occupation % age
Crop farming	36	94.74	4	15.38	—	—
Dairy farming	2	5.26	14	53.85	—	—
Fishing	—	—	—	—	—	—
Vegetable farming	—	—	2	7.69	5	71.42
Poultry farming	—	—	—	—	—	—
Piggeries	—	—	—	—	—	—
Service	—	—	4	15.38	1	14.29
Labour	—	—	1	3.85	—	—
Others	—	—	1	3.85	1	14.29
Total	38	100.00	26	100.00	7	100.00

Shaikh and their Primary Occupations

In fact there is no caste system among Muslims. In whatever form it is found among them, it is the gift of Indian soil. Among Muslims there are two main sects-Sunni and Shia. Except these-two, the other titles of Muslims are on the basis of the community or leader, they are following, and within it also there are variation and complexities. For example, the Indian muslims who claim their linkages with 'quraish'—a community of Saudi Arabia to which Prophet Muhammad (Peace be on him) belonged, call them 'quraishi' or those who establish their linkage with Hazrat Farooq or Hazrat Siddique—the two calips, call them as Farooqi or Siddiqui respectively. But in India Muslims are also divided on the basis of their occupation such as Quazi who use to be judge during the Muslim rule. The caste of converted Muslims is also according to their original Hindu caste. For example, Rajput converts call them Pathan or Khan but migrants of Afghanistan also call them Pathan. However, since the number of Muslim respondents was not large, all the Muslim respondents have been put under one category and are called Shaikhs here. Therefore, whenever the term Shaikh has been used with reference to caste, it includes all the Muslim respondents.

Since the Muslims of all categories have been included in Shaikh, there is a wide range of occupation among them. Except in piggeries due to the religious bar, Shaikh have all the occupations selected for the present study (Table VI). Crop farming is quite popular among Shaikhs and 74 respondents or 87 per cent of total have it as their first, second or third occupation. About 67 per cent respondents have crop farming as their first occupation. It is their main source of livelihood. A reasonable percentage of Shaikh respondents are economically well of and have large size of holdings. They produce wheat, rice, sugarcane and oilseed for commercial purposes. There are 12 respondents accounting 16 per cent of respondents in the category who have crop farming as their second occupation, while only 5 respondents have it as third occupation. Majority of the Shaikh respondents are very efficient crop farmer. With their moderate level of knowledge and involvement, they produce better crops of wheat, rice, and sugarcane. Crop farming is their hereditary occupation which also help them in increasing crop productivity.

Poultry farming is also very common among Shaikh engaging about 59 per cent of the respondents. Earlier it was considered to be women's job who use to do it as side occupation to support the family. By and large it was common among low caste Muslims. But now due to the changed dietary habit of large percentage of pupulation, the poultry products are in great demand. Hence, in rural areas in general and in villages lying near towns in particular, poultry farming has gained popularity. Several young enterprising respondents have started their modern poultry farms, and poultry farming as domestic occupation has also considerably expanded. It has remained no longer a women's job but men are taking great interest in it and a large number of them are doing it.

There are only 6 respondent who are having dairy farming as their main occupation and they do it on commercial basis, while 19 respondents or more than one-fourth under this category have it as their second occupation. Still the larger number of Shaikh respondents accounting 29 per cent of the total respondents, are under this catergory. Dairy farming is favourite occupation of Muslims who were basically nomads. It is a major source of income for Gujar, Gadaria, and Banjara who are, by and large, Muslims. But among those Muslims who are included in Shaikh, dairy farming is important primary occupation engaging about 48 per cent Shaikh respondents as their first, second and third occupation. There are only 8 respondents with dairy farming as their first occupation, while 23 respondents, acoounting 31 per cent of the respective category have it as second and third occupation. Twenty seven per cent of total Shaikhs have dairy farming as their second occupation.

TABLE VI

Shaikhs and the'r Primary Occupations

Occupations	*First No. of Respon*	*Occupation % age*	*Second No. of Respon*	*Occupation % age*	*Third No. of Respon*	*Occvpation % age*
Crop farming	57	67.07	12	16.00	5	9.62
Dairy farming	8	9.41	23	30.67	8	15.38
Fishing	—	—	3	4.00	8	15.38
Vegetable farming	1	1.18	8	10.67	6	11.54
Poultry farming	6	7.06	19	25.33	25	48.08
Piggeries	—	—	—	—	—	—
Services	2	2.35	5	6.67	—	—
Labour	9	10.59	2	2.66	—	—
Others	2	2.34	3	4.00	—	—
Total	85	100.00	75	100.00	52	100.00

In both the above categories, they do it on commercial and subsistence basis. There are 8 rerpondents who have it as their third occupation mainly on subsistence basis. Dairy farming is the main occupation of some of the respondents, and it is their hereditary occupation. But substantial number of Shaikh respondents do it on subsistence basis, and the quantity of dairy product is low.

Vegetable farming is not a favourite occupation of Shaiks. They do it mainly on subsistence basis. There is a single respondent who has vegetable farming as his first occupation, while 8 and 6 respondents have it as their second and third occupation respectively. The only vegetable grown by the Shaikhs on commercial basis is potato. Shaikhs, being non-vegetarian, are also interested in fishing but it is not their main occupation. There is not a single shaikh with fishing as his first occupation. There are three Shaikhs having fishing as second occupation, while 8 respondents accouting 15 per cent in this group, have fishing as their third occupation. They practice fishing on subsistence basis. The fishing is practiced by low caste Muslims.

About 27 per cent Shaikhs are in service, labour and other occupations. Nearly 13 per cent are in labour and 8 per cent in service. They have these occupations as their first and second occupation. There are only two Shaikhs with service as their first occupation, while among 5 it is second occupation. Roughly 10 per cent Shaikhs have labour as their first occupation, while two have it as second occupation. A close look at the questionnaire shows that poor Muslims are under these categories.

Kurmis and their Primary Occupations

Kurmi is a caste mainly found in Central and Eastern Uttar Pradesh. It is a very hard working efficient farming caste. The agricultural productivity among Kurmis is more. They, in fact, know how to conserve their agricultural resources. Crop farming

TABLE VII

Kurmis and their Primary Occupations

Occupations	*First No. of Respon*	*Occupation % age*	*Second No. of Respon*	*Occupation % age*	*Third No. of Respon*	*Occupation % age*
Crop farming	39	79.59	6	22.43	2	11.76
Dairy farming	3	6.12	9	32.14	4	23.53
Fishing	—	—	—	—	1	5.88
Vegetable farming	—	—	8	28.58	9	52.95
Poultry farming	—	—	—	—	—	—
Piggeries	—	—	—	—	—	—
Service	3	6.13	1	3.57	—	—
Labour	2	4.08	2	7.14	1	5.88
Others	2	4.08	2	7.14	—	—
Total	49	100.00	28	100.00	17	100.00

is their main occupation, engaging about 96 per cent of the total Kurmis (Table VII). Out of this, nearly 80 per cent have crop farming as their first occupation, while 6 and 2 respondents have it as their second and third occupation. They grow mostly wheat and rice and sell substantial portion of it. Dairy farming is another occupation popular among Kurmis. There are only 3 respondents accounting nearly 6 per cent of the total respondents, who have dairy farming as their first occupation, but the larger number has it as second occupation. There are [illegible] respondents constituting nearly one-third of the respondents under this category. Four respondents have it as their third occupation. Kurmis are also known for vegetable farming especially onion and potato but incidently it has not emerged as their first occupation. But about 35 per cent Kurmi respondents have vegetable farming as their second and third occupation. Eight respondents accounting nearly 29 per cent respondents, are in former, while 9 respondents accounting 53 per cent of the respondents, are in the latter group. They are, by and large, vegetarian caste and none of them practice poultry farming and piggeries. There is a single respondent having fishing as his third occupation.

Nearly 27 respondents are engaged in service, labour and other occupations. There are 3 respondents in service which is their main occupation, while one respondent has it as secondary occupation. Kurmis are in better services. Labour is first and second occupation of 4 respondents two falling in each category, while one respondent has it as his third occupation. Generally they are agricultural labourers with few exceptions.

Ahirs and their Primary Occupations

Ahirs trace their descent from the God Krishna whose relations with milkmaids of Brindaban play an important part in Hindu mythology. Lord Krishna himself belonged to a nomadic caste who grazes cattle and makes butter (Risley,

1969). However, Ahirs are famous all over Uttar Pradesh for their dairy farming. It is their hereditary occupation. Among the selected Ahir respondents the similar trend has emerged. Out of 139 Ahir respondents 122 have dairy farming as their first, second and third occuation (Table VIII). It accounts roughly 88 per cent of the total Ahir respondents. Nearly 54 per cent of the total respondents have dairy farming as their first occupation, while 40 respondents, accounting more than 30 per cent respondents of the group, have it as their second occupation. There are 7 repondents having dairy as their third occupation. Ahirs are professional dairy farmers and it is their hereditary occupation. They are better knowledgeable and skilled persons in this respect. As a result the amount of dairy product among Ahir respondents is more as compared to the respondents of the other castes. However, by and large, they practice it on commercial basis. They sell raw milk as well as dairy products. In several villages they take out the butter and sell the skinned milk on barter system. The dairy farming, on the one hand, is expanding around the city centres, while on the other, it is declining in far away villages. Increasing demand of the dairy product is basic reason for the former, while deforestation and shrinking of grazing and pasture lands is the cause of the latter. But recently Government has started giving highly subsidised loan for dairy farming which may give a boost to this occupation, although the loan is highly misutilised.

As a result of shrinking of grazing and pasture lands affecting dairy farming adversely, crop farming among Ahirs has gained popularity. Nearly 93 per cent Ahir respondents have crop farming as either first, second or third occupation. Fifty respondents have crop farming as their first occupation, while 69 respondents amounting to nearly 53 per cent of the respondents of the group, have it as their second occupation. An other 10 respondents, constituting nearly 17 per cent respondents of the group have it as their third occupation.

TABLE VIII

Ahirs and their Primary Occupations

Occupations	*First No. of Respon*	*Occupation % age*	*Second No. of Respon*	*Occupation % age*	*Third No. of Respon*	*Occupation % age*
Crop farming	50	35.97	69	52.68	10	16.67
Dairy farming	75	53.96	40	30.53	7	11.67
Fishing	—	—	—	—	1	1.67
Vegetable farming	3	2.16	14	10.69	18	30.00
Poultry farming	—	—	1	0.76	—	—
Piggeries	—	—	—	—	—	—
Service	3	2.16	1	0.76	19	31.67
Labour	8	5.75	6	4.58	5	8.32
Others	—	—	—	—	—	—
Total	139	100.00	131	100.00	60	100.00

Ahirs grow variety of crops but emphasis varies from region to region.

Majority of Ahirs are vegetarian. Hence, they do not practice poultry, fishing and piggeries but there are two exceptions viz. one Ahir has fishing as his third occupation, while the other one has poultry farming as his second occupation. However, since they are basically vegetarian, more than onefourth of Ahir respondents are engaged vegetable farming as their either first, second or third occupation. Due to dominance of crop farming and doing farming as first occupation, only 3 respondents, have vegetable farming as their first occupation, but 14 respondents, accounting nearly 11 per cent respondents of the group, have vegetable farming as second occupation, while 18 respondents have it as their third occupation. They practice it on commercial as well as subsistence basis. They grow potatoes, onion and several kind of green vegetables.

About 30 per cent of Ahir respondents are in service and labour. The former covers nearly 16 per cent, while the latter 14 per cent. Service is main occupation of three respondents, while only one respondent has it as second occupation. There are 19 respondents, constituting nearly 32 per cent respondents of the group, with service as their third occupation. Some Ahirs are in military and administrative jobs, while majority is in clerical job. A few Ahirs are teachers as well. Nearly 6 per cent Ahir respondents have it as their second and third occupation respectively. They are either agricultural workers or freelance labourers doing whatever job they get at required time.

Pasis and their Primary Occupations

Pasi—a Dravidian tribe, is a backward caste found mostly in Central Uttar Pradesh. It is hard working, very efficient caste. There is, by and large, no religious and socio-cultural taboos in adoption of occupations. Hence, they emerged in all the selected occupations in this study. Crop farming is their major occupation engaging nearly 83 per cent of the total Pasi respondents (Table IX). Thirty eight respondents, accounting 55 per cent of total respondents have crop farming as their first occupation, while 16 respondents, amounting nearly 31 per cent of the respondents of this group have it as their second occupation. Only 3 respondents have it as third occupation. Pasis grow variety of crops and their crop productivity is high. Their entire family works in the field throughout the day and some times in the late evening and early morning.

Vegetable farming is also quite popular among Pasis. It engages nearly 58 per cent respondents. They are professional growers of vegetables and have age long experience in it. They know every detail of vegetable cultivation. Hence, the yield per unit of area and labour is high among Pasi respondents. They mostly grow green vegetables. However, it is main occupation of 13 respondents who account nearly 19 per cent of the total. Large number of Pasis have vegetable farming as their second occupation. There are 26 respondents, accounting 50 per cent respondents of this group, under this category. There is a single respondent with vegetable farming as his third occupation. Pasis grow vegetables mainly for selling purposes. A part from potato and onion, they grow variety of seasonal green vegetables and sell it by themselves. They sell vegetables on cash as well as on barter system. Some times Pasis purchase vegetables from higher caste people and sell it.

Although fishing is not their main occupation, it is second and third occupation of nearly 12 per cent Pasi respondents. There are 4 respondents in each, group but in the former it accounts nearly 8 per cent of this group, while in latter it constitutes about 27 per cent respondents in the group. They mainly do it on subsistence basis. Besides this, they are in poultry farming and piggeries as well. Piggeries is main occupation of one

TABLE IX

Pasis and their Primary Occupations

Occupations	*First No. of Respon*	*Occupation % age*	*Second No. of Respon*	*Occupation % age*	*Third No. of Respon*	*Occupation % age*
Crop farming	38	55.07	16	30.77	3	20.01
Dairy farming	—	—	2	3.85	3	20.01
Fishing	—	—	4	7.69	4	26.67
Vegetable farming	13	18.84	26	50.00	1	6.67
Poultry farming	—	—	1	1.92	1	6.67
Piggeries	1	1.45	—	—	1	6.67
Service	—	—	1	1.92	2	13.30
Labour	15	21.74	2	3.85	—	—
Others	2	2.90	—	—	—	—
Total	69	100.00	52	100.00	15	100.00

respondent, while the other one has it as his third occupation. Similarly in poultry farming there are only 2 respondents. One has it as his second occupation, while the other one as his third occupation.

Nearly 27 per cent Pasi respondents are in service, labour and other occupations but about one-fourth are labourers. About 22 per cent Pasis are labourers and it is their main occupation. They are either agricultural workers or freelancing labourers working in construction, earthwork, etc. However, their economic condition is poor. Only 2 respondents have labour as their second occupation, while there is none having it as third occupation. There are only 3 Pasis in service, having it as their second or third occupation. Out of it one is a school teacher, while the other two are peons.

Kachhis and their Primary Occupations

Kachhi is a caste similar to Kori or Pasi. It is a tribe of opium grower and market gardener (Crooke, 1974). It is a low caste, and the people are generally poor. Crop farming and vegetable farming is their main occupation. Nearly 57 per cent respondents have crop farming as their first occupation. There is little diversity in their occupation. There is none having crop farming as second or third occupation. Vegetable farming is second important occupation among Kachhis. They are professional vegetable growers and sellers. It is main occupation of one respondent, while 2 respondents have it as second occupation. They mostly do it for selling purposes. They sometimes purchase and seli vegetables. Dairy farming is not very popular among Kachhis but nevertheless 3 respondents amounting nearly one-fifth respondents, have it second or third occupation. Interestingly dairy farming is the only third occupation among Kachhis. Nearly 29 per cent Kachhi respondents are labourers and it is their first occupation. They are either agricultural labourers or working in construction and earthwork. There is a single Kachhi in service and he is a peon in a local primary schools.

TABLE X

Kachhis and their Primary Occupations

Occupations	*First No. of Respon*	*Occupation % age*	*Second No. of Respon*	*Occupation % age*	*Third No. of Respon*	*Occupation*
Crop farming	8	57.14	—	—	—	—
Dairy farming	—	—	1	33.33	2	100.00
Fishing	—	—	—	—	—	—
Vegetable farming	1	7.14	2	66.67	—	—
Poultry farming	—	—	—	—	—	—
Piggeries	—	—	—	—	—	—
Service	1	7.14	—	—	—	—
Labour	4	28.58	—	—	—	—
Others	—	—	—	—	—	—
Total	14	100.00	3	100.00	2	100 00

Lodh and their Primary Occupations

Lodh is a very low caste but they are very hefty and efficient. There is no religious bar in adopting any occupation except piggeries, but crop farming and fishing is their main occupation. Nearly 82 per cent lodhs have crop farming as their first occupation which accounts about 59 per cent of total respondents (Table XI). They practice crop farming on subsistence basis and grow mostly foodgrains. There are 2 respondents with crop farming as their second occupation. A similar number has crop farming as their third occupation but they account one-third respondents under this group. Fishing is second major occupation, and it is the first occupation of nearly 12 per cent respondents, while about 30 per cent respondents have it as their second occupation. Three respondents, accounting 50 per cent respondents of the group, have fishing as their third occupation. It is their commercial cum subsistence occupation. They sell it in cash or through barter system. It provides major support to their living. There is a single respondent having poultry farming as his second occupation. About 65 per cent respondents are in labour and service. it is a poor caste. Hence, nearly 47 per cent respondents have labour either as their first or second occuption. Five respondents, constituting nearly 30 per cent of Lodh respondents, have labour as their first occupation, while 3 respondents constututing about 18 per cent of the group, have it as their second occupation. There are only 3 respondents in service. Out of it 2 have it as their second occupation, while one has it as third occupation. One is a school teacher, while 2 are peon in other organisation.

Koirs and their Primary Occupations

Koirs (Also spelled as 'Koeri, or Koari') are low caste Hindus and are similar to Kachhi of Central Uttar Pradesh. They are mostly found in Eastern Uttar Pradesh. They are known as vegetable grower. They are most efficient vegetable growers and it is their hereditary occupation. They devote a small portion

TABLE XI

Lodh and their Primary Occupations

Occupations	*First No. of Respon.*	*Occupation % age*	*Second No. of Respon.*	*Occupation % age*	*Third No. of Respon.*	*Occupation % age*
Crop farming	10	58.85	2	11.76	2	33.33
Dairy farming	—	—	2	11.76	—	—
Fishing	2	11.76	5	29.43	3	50.00
Vegetable farming	—	—	2	11.76	—	—
Poultry farming	—	—	2	11.76	—	—
Piggeries	—	—	—	—	—	—
Service	—	—	2	11.76	1	16.67
Labour	5	29.41	3	17.65	—	—
Others	—	—	—	—	—	—
Total	17	100.00	17	100.00	6	100.00

of their land for vegetable farming, and it is called '*Bari or Behra*. They remain busy in it throughout the year producing one vegetable or the other. However, 50 per cent of the total Kori respondents have vegetable farming as their first occuption, while 3 respondents have it as third occupation. They not only cultivate and sell vegetables but also purchase and resell in the villages and also in local weekly markets. It is their main occupation and source of livelihood. Crop farming is the second important occupation of Koris, being first occupation of 4 respondents or nearly 22 per cent of the total. There are 7 respondents, accounting 50 per cent respondents of this group, who have crop farming as their second occupation. There are 2 respondents with crop farming as their third occupation. Hence, crop farming altogether engages nearly 72 per cent of total respondents. Among Koris crop farming is subsistence type and they grow mainly food crops.

Dairy farming is also popular among Koris constituting 50 per cent of total respondents with either first, second or third occupation. There is single respondent with dairy farming as his first occupation while there are 2 and 6 respondents having it as their second and third occupation respectively. They constitute nearly 14 and 60 per cent of respondent in their groups. They practice it on subsistence and commercial basis. Koris are purely vegetarian and they are locally known as *Bhagat*. Hence, fishing, poultry farming and puggeries are totally absent among them. And, perhaps, this is the reason that they are quite acceptable and popular vegetable grower and seller among all castes.

They are, by and large, poor. Hence, the large percentage work as labourer. Labour is main occupation of nearly 17 per cent respondents. There is one respondent with labour as second occupation and similar number has it as third occupation. Service is not popular among Koris. There are 2 respondents

TABLE XII

Koris and their Primary Occupations

Occupations	*First No. of Respon*	*Occupation % age*	*Second No. of Respon*	*Occupation % age*	*Third No. of Respon*	*Occupation % age*
Crop farming	4	22.22	7	50.00	2	2.00
Dairy farming	1	5.56	2	14.29	6	60.00
Fishing	—	—	—	—	—	—
Vegetable farming	9	50.00	3	21.43	—	—
Poultry farming	—	—	—	—	—	—
Piggeries	—	—	—	—	—	—
Service	—	—	1	7.14	1	10.00
Labour	3	16.66	1	7.14	1	10.00
Others	1	5.76	—	—	—	—
Total	18	100.00	14	100.00	10	100.00

in service. One is a teacher, while the other is peon in the same school.

Nomadic Caste and their Primary Occupations

Generally *Gujar*, *Banjara* and *Gadaria* are nomads. They move with their flock of animals and all belongings from one place to other. But due to the technological change, modernisation and shrinkage of grazing and pasture lands, they have started sedentary life. However, due to their mobile nature, they have been put together and are called Nomadic Caste although in census they are given separately. Their total number is also very small. Crop farming and dairy farming are their main occupations. The former is generally practiced by sedentary population, while the latter by nomadic. Crop farming is the main occupation of 8 respondents who constitute nearly 57 per cent respondents, while a single respondent has it as second occupation. There are 8 respondents accounting nearly 43 per cent with dairy farming as first occupation, while there are 9 respondents constituting 60 per cent respondents of this group within it as their second occupation. A single respondent has it as third occupation. They are absent in vegetable farming, service and piggeriers. There are 2 respondents in fishing and equal number is in poultry farming, having their second and third occupation. Three respondents are labourers and it is their second occupation. They are engaged in various kind of labours.

Other Castes and their Primary Occupations

Besides above discussed castes, there are other castes such as vaishyas, Kumhar, Carpenter and Barber who are very small in number. Hence, they are grouped together under 'other castes' which together account about 2 per cent of total respondents. Crop farming and dairy farming are their main occupations. There is none in poultry farming and piggeries, while there are only 2 respondents in fishing—one each having first and third

TABLE XIII

Nomadic castes and their Primary Occupation

Occupations	*First No. of Respon.*	*Occupation % age*	*Second No. of Respon.*	*Occupation % age*	*Third No. of Respon.*	*Occupation % age*
Crop farming	8	57.14	1	6.67	—	—
Dairy farming	6	42.86	9	60.00	1	33.33
Fishing	—	—	1	6.67	1	33.34
Vegetable farming	—	—	—	—	—	—
Poultry farming	—	—	1	6.66	1	33.33
Piggeries	—	—	—	—	—	—
Service	—	—	—	—	—	—
Labour	—	—	3	20.00	—	—
Others	—	—	—	—	—	—
Total	14	100.00	15	100.00	3	100.00

occupation. Crop farming engages 18 respondents accounting nearly 64 per cent of total respondents as first and second occupations. There are 15 respondents constituting nearly 54 per cent of total who have crop farming as their first occupation, while 3 respondents were having it as their second occupation.

Dairy farming has a wider coverage. It is being adopted as first, second or third occupation by 17 respondents, while 4 respondents have it as first occupation. Seven respondents are practicing it as their second occupation accounting about 41 per cent respondents in the group. There are 6 respondents constituting half of the respondents of the group who have dairy farming as their third occupation. A large percentage of these castes are in service, labour and other occupations, which together engage nearly 54 per cent of total respondents. Out of this, only 3 are in service, 4 are labourers, and the remaining are in other occupations.

Conclusion and Suggestions

The following points clearly emerge out of the above discussion of caste and primary occupations :

(i) Crop farming is the main occupation in the state. The similar pattern emerges in the analysis of caste and pripary occupations. Nearly 57.3, 21.2 and 5.1 per cent respondents have crop farming as first, second and third occupations respectively. Crop farming is the main occupation of high caste respondents. They grow fine grains and more remunerative crops as they produce them for selling purposes. On the contrary, low caste respondents grow course grains and produce it on subsistence basis. Similarly there is a considerable difference in agricultural production also. The agricultural productivity, by and large, is higher among

TABLE XIV

Other Castes and their Primary Occupations

Occupations	*First No. of Respon*	*Occupation % age*	*Second No. of Respon*	*Occupation % age*	*Third No. of Respon*	*Occupation % age*
Crop farming	15	53.57	3	17.65	—	—
Dairy farming	4	14.29	7	41.18	6	50.00
Fishing	1	3.57	—	—	1	8.33
Vegetable farming	—	—	1	5.88	3	25.00
Poultry farming	—	—	—	—	—	—
Piggeries	—	—	—	—	—	—
Services	1	3.57	—	—	2	16.67
Labour	3	10.71	1	5.89	—	—
Others	4	14.29	5	29.41	—	—
Total	28	100.00	17	100.00	12	100.00

high caste respondents as compared to low caste respondents.

(ii) Dairy farming is next important occupation engaging 380 respondents with their either first, second, or third occupation. Out of this nearly 27.6 per cent have dairy farming as their first occupation, while 47.6 and 21.3 per cent have it as their second and third occupation respectively. Dairy farming, by and large, is main occupation of Ahirs, although the other castes also practice is but mainly on subsistence basis. Ahirs practice dairy farming on commercial basis. Nearly one-third of total respondents engaged in dairy farming as their first, second or third occupation are Ahirs. Among the Ahir respondents nearly 88 per cent are engaged in dairy farming as their first, second, or third occupation. Out of this nearly 54 per cent have it as their first occupation, while about 29 and 5 per cent have it as second and third occupation respectively. Even among Ahir respondents with dairy farming, nearly 61 per cent have it as first occupation, and 33 and 6 per cent as second and third occupation respectively. Besides occupational hierarchy, there is variation in dairy products also. The production per unit of animal or per head is higher among Ahir respondents as compared to the respondents of the other castes who practice dairy farming. Ahir respondents know the art of keeping dairy cattle, whereas the respondents of the other castes lack it. He is also almost a semi-doctor various diseases of dairy animals.

(iii) Vegetable farming ranks third in terms of number of respondents engaged. There are 259 respondents accounting 25.07 per cent of total respondents who have vegetable farming as first, second or third occupation. Nearly 14.29 per cent have vegetable farming as their first occupation, while 52.51 and 333.20 per cent have it as their second and third occupations respectively. Vegetable farming has got considerable changed especially around urban centres. People of different castes have started it. But still in rural areas, especially in remote parts, it is more popular among Kachhi, Kori, Kurmi and Pasi. Nearly 28 per cent of total respondent engaged in vegetable farming as their first, second and third occupation, belong to these castes. About 48 per cent respondents of these castes have vegetable farming as their first, second and third occupation. Out of this, nearly 32 per cent have dairy farming as their first occupation, whereas 54 per cent and 14 per cent have it as their second and third occupations respectively. The respondents of these castes know the minute detail of vegetable farming. And, therefore, the quality and production of vegetable in the fields of these respondents is better and more as compared to the respondents of the other castes.

(iv) By and large, poultry farming is practiced by Shaikhs and that too by low caste people. The other castes who practice poultry farming belong to lower castes. Nearly 59 per cent Shaikh respondents have poultry farming as their first, second or third occupation, and they constitute nearly 74 per cent of the respondents practicing poultry farming. However, among the poultry farming shaikh respondents 12 per cent have it as first occupation, while 38 and 55 per cent practice it as their second and third occupation respectively.

(v) Piggeries is the main occupation of Scheduled Castes. It is rarely practiced by the respondents of the other castes. Nearly 58 per cent Scheduled Castes have piggeries as their first, second or third occupation. They constitute nearly 98 per cent respondents practicing this occupation. Among the piggeries practicing respondents, nearly 53 per cent have it as their first occupation, while 41 and 6 per cent have it as second and third occupation respectively. Fishing is common among low castes whether they belong to Hindu or Muslim religion. Scheduled Castes, Lodh and low caste Muslims have it as their first, second or third occupation.

(vi) The poor respondents of higher castes in general and the respondents of low castes in particular, are labourers. They work as agricultural labourer, or freelancing labourers. The Scheduled Castes dominate the scene. Nearly 43 per cent Scheduled Caste respondents are labourers having it as their primary, secondary or tertiary source of income. They constitute nearly 51 per cent of total labourer respondents. Among the Scheduled Caste labourer respondents, 70 per cent have it as main source of livelihood, while 29 and only one per cent have it as their secondary and tertiary source of income respectively.

(vii) Substantial percentage of respondents in service belong to higher castes especially Brahmin, Shaikh and Rajputs. A minor percentage of lower caste respondents are in service. A further analysis of respondents in service indicates that higher caste respondents are in superior and better jobs (white collar jobs), while lower caste respondents are in inferior and ministerial services.

References

Alexander, J.W., 1963 : *Economic Geography*, New Jersey.

Barth, F. : The 1960 : The System of Social Stratification in Sawat, North Pakistan in E.R. Leach (Ed.) *Aspect, of Castes in South India, Ceylone, and N.W. Pakistan.*

Buchanan, R.G. 1959 : Some Reflections on Agricultural Geography, *Annals of the Association of American Geographers*, Vol. 44.

Bailey, F.G. 1963 : Closed Social Stratification in India, *European Journal of Sociology*, No. 1 Vol. XIV.

Berreman, G.D. 1967 : Stratifications, Pluralism and Interaction : A Comparative Analysis of Caste, in Reuch, A.D. and Knight, J. (Eds.) *Caste and Race*, London.

Beteille, A. 1965 : *Caste, Class and Power*, California.

——— 1961 : Closed and Open Stratification, *European Journal of Sociology*, Vol. VII.

——— 1969 : The Politics of Non-Antagonistic Strata, *Contribution to Indian Sociology*.

——— 1974 : *Studies in Agrarain Social Structure*, OUP, London.

Bhat A, 1975 : *Caste, Class and Politics*, Delhi.

Berry, B.J.L. et. al. 1976 : *The Geography of Economic Systems*, New Jersey.

Crooke, W., 1974 : *The Tribes and Castes of the Northern India* Vol. I-IV.

Caplo, T., 1954 : *The Sociology of Work*, Illinois.

Dutta, N.K. 1931 : *Origin and Growth of Caste in India*, Calcutta.

Dore, R.P. 1958 : *City Life in Japan : A Study of Tokyo Ward*, Berkely.

Ghurye, G.S. 1961 : *Caste, Class and Occupation*, Bombay.

Grigg, D.B. 1974 : *The Agricultural Systems of the World : An Evolutionary Approach*, London.

——— 1984 : *An Introduction to Agricultural Geography*, London.

Gadgril, D.R. 1945 : *Poona ; A Socio-economic Survey*, Part I & II.

Risley, H.H. *The People of India*, 2nd Ed. Delhi.

Jones, C. E. & Darkehwald, G.G., 1962 : *Economic Geography*, New York.

Kahi, J.A. 1957 : *The American Caste Structure*.

Kosambi, D.D. & Sharma R.S. (Eds) 1958 : *Indian Society, Historical Probings in Memory of D.D. Kosambi*, New Delhi.

Kumar, A. 1985 : *Impact of Caste on Primary Occupation* (Unpublished M.A. Dissertation, Delhi University).

Leach, E.R. (Ed) 1960 : *Aspects of Caste to South India, Ceylone and North West Pakistan*, Cambridge.

Louis Dumont : *Home-Hierarchicus : The Caste System and its Implications* (Trans. Marx Samisbury)

Mohammad, N. 1978 : *Agricultural Land Use in India*, Delhi.

——— 1981 : *Perspectives in Agricultural Geography*, Volume I to V. Delhi.

——— 1981 : Socio-economic Determinants of Diffusion of Agricultural Innovation, in N. Mohammad, (Ed.), *Perspectives in Agricultural Geography*, Vol. III.

Mukherjee, A.B. 1980 : *The Chamars of Uttar Pradesh*, Delhi.

Nesfield, J.C. : *Caste System of North Western Provinces and Oudh.*

Nijhawan, P. 1986 : *Impact of Caste on Primary Occupation* (Unpublished M.A. Dissertation, Delhi University).

Omvedt, G. (Ed.) 1982 : *Land, Caste and Politics in Indian States*, Delhi.

Pandit, M. 1979 : Caste and Class in Maharashtra, *Economic and Political Weekly*, Annual No. XIV, No. 780.

Risley, H.H. 1969 : *The People of India*, 2nd Ed. Delhi.

Russed, R.V. & Lal, H. 1975 : *The Tribes and Castes of Central Provinces of India*, Vol. I-IV (Reprint).

Schwartzberg, J.E. 1965 : The Distribution of Selected Caste in the North Indian Plain, *Geographical Review*, Vol. 45, No. 4.

——— 1968 : Caste Regions of the Northern Indian Plains, in Singer, M. & Bernard, S.H. (Eds.) *Structure and Change in Indian Society*, Chicago.

Schwartzberg, J.E. 1978: *A Historical Atlas of South East Asia*, London.

Sinhas, S. 1982 : *Caste System : Myths, Reality Challange*, New Delhi.

Sharma, R.S. 1958 : *Sudras in Ancient India*, Delhi.

Sharma, K.K. 1984 : *Impact of Caste on Primary Occupations* (Unpublished M.A. Dissertation, Delhi University).

Sharma, D.D. 1983 : *Impact of Caste on Primary Occupations* (Unpublished M.A. Dissertation, Delhi University).

Singh, Y. 1968 : Caste and Class : Some Aspects of Continiuty and Change, *Sociological Bulletin*, No. 2, Vol. XVII.

Srinivas, M.N. 1966 : *Social Change in Modern India*, Berkeley.

Singh, J. 1970 : *Agricultural Atlas of India : A Geographical Analysis*, Kurukshetra.

Singh, R. : Agrarian Social Structure and Peasant Unrest : A Study in Land Grab Movement in Basti, East U.P., *Sociological Bulletin*, No. 23.

Sharma, K.L. 1972 : Levels of Mobility in Caste Structure : A Hypothetical Refinement, *The Indian Journal of Social Work*, Vol. XXXII.

Thoman, R.S. et. at. 1968 : *The Geography of Economic Activity*, New York.

TWO

Sex Disparity in Scheduled Caste Literacy in Maharashtra : A Case of Selected Villages

Dr. Krishan Chand Ramotra

The term 'literacy' is that qualitative attribute of population which is undisputedly one of the sensitive indices of progress for society as a whole and essential pre-condition for raising the status of individual deprived and unprivileged communities such as the Scheduled Castes and Scheduled Tribes within it. The country like India is not only characterised by low level of literacy but also caste and sex disparities. The sex disparity in literacy is not uncommon in Indian society but such differentials are more acute and alarming among the Schedule Castes. This sort of inequality in education is not recent phenomenon; in fact a historical legacy of Bramhanical supremacy in India. Manu, the law giver had a low opinion of women in general and the Scheduled Castes in particular. "The triumphant Bramhanism bengan its onslaught on both the Shudras and the women in pursuit of the old ideal servility and Bramhanism did succeed in making the shudras and women the servile classes, shudras the serfs to three higher classes (i.e., Bramhan, Kshatriya and Vaishya) and women serfs to their husbands," (Ambedkar,

1987, p. 316). Women in general and Scheduled Castes in particular had no right to study the Vedas which stood for education during the olden times. Since Independence some steps were initiated to raise the status of females in the Indian Society but consistent male chauvinism has affected the social and economic status of women. Therefore, "in every district, male literacy is higher than female literacy in both rural and urban population" (Sopher, 1980, p. 133).

Now this male dominance is at a declining trend although at a very slow rate. The virtual absence of literacy among females particularly among the Scheduled Caste females until recent was times, the product of such a long continued prejudice against the education of women.

The ma in concern of the present paper is to measure and analyse the male-female disparity in the scheduled caste literacy in Maharashtra based on the 1981 census. The attempt is also made to study the same aspect at micro-regional level i.e. village level. This part of the study is pertained to primary data collected personally by conducting interviews with detailed questionnaires during sample field survey made in February 1987. The selection of three villages is based on the minimum 10 per cent Scheduled Caste population in each village. Secondly, they should form a contiguous region near a town. Accordingly such villages viz. Pimplegaon Kh., Siddhanerli and Vhannur located near Kagal town in the northern part of Kagal taluka of Kolhapur district are selected for the present study. This is conducted to ascertain whether disparity in literacy increases or decreases from macro to micro level.

Methodology

In order to measure the male-female disparity in literacy Sopher's (1974) disparity index has been used.

Sopher's Disparity Index is defined as given below

$$Ds = \log (x_2/x_1) + \log (100 - x_1)/(100 - x_2)$$

$$x_2 > x_1$$

Where x_1 and x_2 are the literacy rates.

An Over View

The literate Scheduled Caste population in Maharashtra is accounted for 35.55 per cent against 21.38 per cent for the same community in India as a whole. It explicates that the position of Maharashtrian Scheduled Castes is better than the same community in the country. On the other hand, when it is compared with the average literacy of Maharashtra State (47.18%) they occupy a far lower position.

The caste system still it has its roots in the Hindu Indian society which divided it into four castes viz. Bramhan, Kshatriya, Vaishya and Shudra. It can be divided into two major groups. First three castes are treated as privileged group (non-scheduled population) and the last (Shudra) un-privileged (Scheduled Caste Community) which was prevented to have access to education. Due to such prejudices the gap between them still exists. It is evident from the 1981 census that 41.30 per cent non-scheduled and 21.55 per cent Scheduled Caste population in India can read and write. The computed disparity index is 0.413. The index is comparatively less in case of Maharashtra (i.e., 0.274) as their literacy rates are higher than the above mentioned figures for the country. For instance, in Maharashtra the literacy percentages are 50.90 and 35.55 for privileged and unprivileged communities respectively.

Male-Female Disparity

The most common form of inequalities are sex disparities in in the socio-economic development of the people—and Maharashtra is not exception to it. Literacy is the most potent weapon which can liberate the females from the traditional exploitation by the male dominance and weaker sections by high caste society. Due to such persistences the sex disparity in the Scheduled Caste literacy was 0.542 against 0.425 for non-scheduled population in Maharashtra in 1981. It indicates the former community lags much behind the later. In case of non-scheduled population the male-female literacy rates are 62.47 per cent and 38.50 per cent against 48.35 per cent and 21.53 per cent for Scheduled Caste males and females respectively as per the 1981 census. It is noticed that the sex disparity in the Scheduled Caste literacy has been mitigated from 0.601 in 1971 to 0.542 in 1981. It shows clearly the progress of female literacy during 1971-81. It also suggests the declining trend of male chauvinism in the society.

Coming down to district level, it is found that districts viz. Jalgaon, Buldhana, Nanded, Parbhani and Aurangabad having high disparity index which is more than 0.644. They form a contiguous region of high disparity in the central part of Maharashtra (Fig. 1). The above mentioned last three districts form a major part of relatively backward Marathwada within it.

On the other hand, the districts with low disparity are—Ratnagiri, Bombay, Thane, Nashik, Ahmednagar, Pune, Amravati, Wardha and Nagpur. The disparity index varies from 0.112 to 0.491. These districts constitute two pockets; one, the western side and the other in the north-eastern part of the state. It is investigated, as the literacy rates of both the sexes come closer to each other the disparity decreases as moderization advances. For instance, the proportion of the Scheduled Caste female literates is 9.09 per cent against 37.98 per cent male in Aurangabad district. With the result of very low female literacy in comparison to male, it has registered highest disparity index of 0.787. On the other hand, Bombay metropolitan with no rural population at all coupled with main centre of industrialization and male-females to a larger extent have equal opportunity to have education, has displayed lowest disparity index (0.396). It further explicates that modernization has made a little if not much dent on the socio-economic development of this down-trodden section of the society.

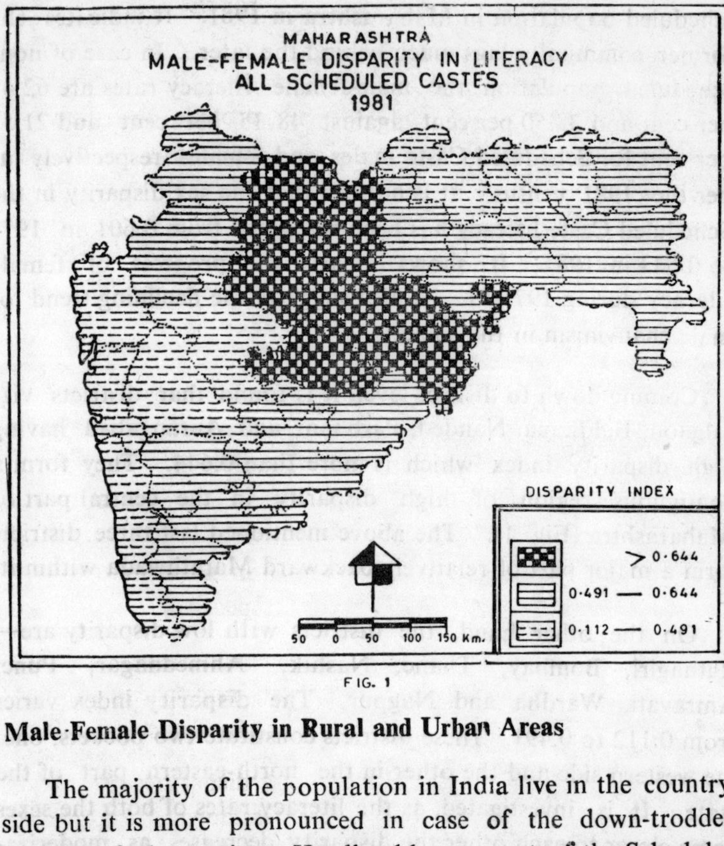

FIG. 1

Male-Female Disparity in Rural and Urban Areas

The majority of the population in India live in the countryside but it is more pronounced in case of the down-trodden section of the society. Hardly 16 per cent of the Scheduled Caste population constitutes urban dwellers against about 23 per cent of total population in India. The corresponding figures for Maharashtra are 32 and 35 respectively. The rural-urban dichotomy itself bring inequality in the developmental processes of people. This inequality in residence further accentuates the disparity in literacy in general and weaker sections in particular since they hardly possess resources. For instance, rural Parbhani has shown highest disparity (0.952) and followed by Aurangabad (0.868), Nanded (0.794) etc. As far as urban area is concerned, the same districts (Aurangabad, Parbhani and Nanded) come under the high disparity index (0.601 to 0.645) but lower than what it is computed for the country-side.

Male-Female Disparity at Village Level

The district census handbooks (1981) provide statistics on the Scheduled Caste and Scheduled Tribe populations by sex only for each village. In 1981 census, the statistics on socio-economic attributes, for instance, literate population, male-female work force for the above mentioned weaker sections particularly at village level as it is in case of total population which is essential for ascertaining their socio-economic status at village level has not been published. Therefore, this part of the paper is based on the primary data collected by conducting the personal interviews with the house-hold members. About 5% sample was collected in the villages viz. Pimplegaon Kh., Siddhanerli and Vhannur located at a distance of 4 kilometers from the nearest town Kagal in Kagal taluka of Kolhhpur district. The proportions of Scheduled Caste population in the above said villages are 25.4, 11.2 and 31.4 per cent respectively.

For each of these villages, the male/female disparity index has separately been computed for total, non-scheduled, and Scheduled Caste populations and presented in Table 1.

It is discerning from this study that disparities in socio-economic attributes increase as one comes down from macro to micro level. At macro level the inequalities remained hiddened whereas at micro-regional levels they are reflected very clearly and significantly. It is evident from Table 1 that male-female variations are significantly sharp both among the non-scheduled and Scheduled Caste populations in Vhannur and Pimplegaon Kh. Almost in all the villages the sex disparity in literacy is very sharp among the Scheduled Castes. It is astonishing to note that the disparity index of the same weaker section

TABLE 1

Male-Female Disparity in Literacy in selected Villages of Kagal Taluka in Kolhapnr District, February 1987

Village/Population	*Average literacy*	*Male literacy*	*Female literacy*	*Male/Female disparity in literacy*
1	2	3	4	5
SIDDNERALI				
Total Population	53.57	61.33	38.66	0.4008
Non-Scheduled Population	65.27	57.44	42.55	0.2600
Scheduled Caste Population	41.17	67.55	32.14	0.6446
VHANNUR				
Total Population	51.81	78.94	21.05	1.1478
Noh-Scheduled Population	50.98	84.61	15.38	1.5808
Scheduled Caste Population	52.54	74.19	25.80	0.9174

1	2	3	4	5
PIMPLEGAON KH.				
Total Population	55.97	72.00	28.00	0.8202
Non-Scheduled Population	57.14	69.64	30.64	0.7275
Scheduled Caste Population	52.77	78.94	21.65	1.1478

is less than the non-scheduled population in Vhannur. This is an exceptional case though this index is higher than Siddhanerli village. It is due to the major differentials in male literacy rates between the Scheduled Caste and non-scheduled populations, otherwise the female literacy in both the sections is deplorably less than the male literacy.

The socio-economic variables also influence the literacy level. In this context, it is found that literacy and education of the children undoubtedly depends upon the education and economic activities of the parents. Hence, there is a strong association between the educated children and educated parents. The illiteracy of the children is associated with illiteracy of the parents engaged in agricultural sector particularly agricultural and landless labourers. It is strongly pronounced in case of female children and uneducated poor parents. It is further investigated that parents engaged in house-hold industries particularly making Kolhapuri *Chapals* having almost literate and educated children.

The village Siddhanerli is identified with low sex disparities in privileged and unprivileged sections of population. It is facilitated with primary and high schools whereas other two villages viz. Vhannur and Pimplegaon Kh. havings schools upto 7th standard only. The availability of schooling facility, location and distance between home and school and prevailing social environment also influence the literacy and education of females.

Conclusion

The sex disparity in the Scheduled Caste literacy is much higher than the corresponding non-scheduled population in Maharashtra. It indicates that women lag behind their men folk but the scheduled caste females are far behind in comparison with the male population of the same community. In this context, the districts viz., Jalgaon, Buldhana, Nanded, Parbhani and

Aurangabad are identified with high sex disparity in Scheduled Caste population. The rural-urban dichotomy, economic backwardness, caste system, illiteracy and ignorance of parents/elderly people affect the literacy of children of both the sexes. It is further noticed that lower is the status of females in the society higher is the sex disparity in literacy. This is specifically true in case of weaker sections in the countryside. It is therefore, necessary to give emphasis on female literacy in general and the Scheduled Castes in particular so as to minimize the sex diparity in it. It will also raise their status in the society.

References

1. Ambedkar, B. (1987), *Writings and Speeches*, Vol. 3, Education Department, Government of Maharashtra, Bombay, p. 316.
2. Sopher, David E. (1974), *A Measure of Disparity*. The Professional Geographer,, Vol. 26, No. 4, pp. 589-92.
3. ————(1980), *Sex Disparity in Indian Literacy*, in Sopher, David E. (ed). An Exploration of India—Geographical Perspective on Society and Culture, Cornell University Press, Ithaca, p. 133.

THREE

Literacy of Scheduled Castes in Bundelkhand Region, U.P. : A Spatial Analysis

Dr. R.K. Shukla and Chunna Singh

Ever since ancient times education has always enjoyed a place of honour in the Indian Society. The history of ancient India is replete with the illumineries of highest thinking, scholarly knowledge and philosophical pursuits. Even today education is accepted to be the most effacious instrument for bringing about a socio-economic change, culminating in the development of the individual and the nation as a whole. It has come to be recognised as a potent needs of national progress, social security and international understanding. It also influences the various attributes of population such as fertility, mortality, mobility, occupations etc. There are surprisingly several paradoxes associated with India and the literacy of her inhabitants. India is relatively a small country but paradoxically having more than 437 million illiterates (1981 Census), and thus, becoming a country distinctly known for the largest number of illiterates in the whole world. There is yet another contradiction related with the number of educational institutions since Independence and the number of illiterates. Despite the tremendous increase in the number of educational institutions, the number of illiterates has shot up from 300 million in 1951 to 437 million in 1981. We have, however, the satisfaction that the percentage of literacy has improved from 16.67% in 1951 to 36.23% in 1981. India is not only characterised by low levels of literacy but also by piercing and startling disparities in the literacy rates between one region and another region, between male and female, between rural and urban areas and between scheduled castes and non-Scheduled Castes.

Even after having multifiaceted constitutional provisions and concessions, the Scheduled castes are the least literate (21.38%) in India as compared to the non-Scheduled Castes (39.01%). Unfortunately regional studies on spatial literacy rates of male-female population of Scheduled Castes and disparity between rural-urban Scheduled Castes and non scheduled castes are still lacking. Hence, in this paper an attempt has been made to assess the spatial patterns and disparity in the level of literacy of Scheduled Castes in the five southern districts of Uttar Pradesh termed as Bundelkhand region of U.P. The study is based on tahsil-wise 1981 census data on literacy.

The region under study lies between 24°11ˢN to 26°27N latitudes and 78° 10'E to 81° 34E longitudes. It is the transition zone between the Ganga plain and the Peninsular India. Administratively, the region is divided into five districts and 22 tahsils having a population of 54,29,075 and area of 29417 Km^2.

Methodology

In order to quantify the magnitude of inequality in literacy Sopher's Disparity Index (Sopher, 1974) as modified by Kundu and Rao (1983) has been used since it satisfies the axioms of additive and multiplicative monotonicity, redistribution and iterative transfers. Sopher's index is as follows :

$$DS = \text{Log}\,(x_2/x_1) + \log\,(100-x_1)/(100-x_2) \ldots\ldots\ldots 1$$

$$x_2 > x_1$$

Sopher's disparity index as modified by Kundu and Rao is given below :

$$DS = \log\,(x_2/x_1) + \text{Log}\,(200-x_1)\,/\,(200-x_2) \ldots\ldots\ldots 2$$

$$x_2 > x_1$$

Or $\text{Log}\,x_2 - \log\,x_1 + \log(200-x_1) - \log\,(200-x_2)\quad x_2 > x_1$

Where, x_1 and x_2 are literacy rates.

This index has three disadvantages—

(*i*) it fails to distinguish between situations by more than two observations,

(*ii*) it violates the DAIA (Decreasing Absolute Inequality Aversion), and

(*iii*) an inability to handle zero (Sopher, 1979). But these snags do not submit any handicap in the present study. The measuring of disparity is potentially a meaningful device to judge quantitatively the degree of spatial diffusion (Ramotra, 1988).

Spatial Patterns of Literacy

The Scheduled castes account 25.60% for Bundelkhand's total population which is higher than the State's average (21.16%). The Scheduled Castes population is predominantly rural (83.96%). The literacy rate among them (17.63%) is much lower in comparison to non-Scheduled Castes (32.82%) in the study region but higher than the State's average (14.69%). Literacy rates on tahsil level have tremendous variations. It is not-able here, that the distributional pattern of Scheduled Castes literacy strongly corresponds to general literacy wherever educational facilities are available sufficiently for general population. The Scheduled Castes have availed themselves accordingly, though not uniformally, nor to the same extent as the non-Scheduled Castes have in many cases. The highest literacy (31.80%) is noticed in Orai tahsil situated in Bundelkhand plain and is followed by Jhansi tahsil (31.38%), whereas the lowest literacy level of 6.67% is found in Mau tahsil of Banda district. (Table—1). There are socio-cultural, economic, historical and political factors responsible for variations in the level of literacy. Taking the region's average (17.63%) as a base, the study region has been divided into following five regions :

(a) Areas of very high literacy rates (26.50%—31.80%)

(b) Areas of high literacy rates (21.20%—26.50%)

(c) Areas of moderate literacy rates (15.90%—21.20%)

(d) Areas of low literacy rates (10.60%—15.90%)

(e) Areas of very low literacy rates (below 10.60%)

Areas of Very High and High Literacy Rates

Areas having literacy rates of 26.50% and above among the scheduled castes cover a total of three tahsils (i.e. Orai, Jhansi and Konch) out of 22 tahsils. Orai and Jhansi tahsils are characterised by he very high literacy rate due to the presence of Orai and Jhansi cities which have a number of educational institutions and commercial and industrial activities. Konch located in Bundelkhand plain has also retained the leading position in literacy due to social awakening (Fig. 1). In these three tahsils the Scheduled Castes male literacy is also very high (above 44%). Jalaun (25.56%) and Moth (23.95%) tahsils have high literacy due to the positive influence of neighbouring cities Orai and Jhansi respectively and social awakening of Scheduled Caste persons.

Areas of Moderate Literacy Rates

There are four tahsils viz. Mauranipur (21.02%), Garautha (20.69%), Hamirpur (18.45%) and Kalpi (17.99%) which manifest moderate literacy rates. Areas of Garautha, Hamirpur and Kalpi tahsils are a prosperous agricultural region whereas Mauranipur is the region of medium size industries where educational facilities helped in the spread of literacy. Besides, the tahsils of moderate literacy are assoicated with moderate level of urbanization.

Areas of Low and Very Low Literacy Rates

In the Central and Southern part of the study region, the seven tahsils namely Banda (15.68%), Rath (15.62%), Maudaha (15.31%), Charakhari (14.00%), Naraini (12.85%), Mahoba (12.73%) and Kulapahar (11.97%) form a contiguous belt of low level of literacy. In these tahsils the male literacy ranges between 20.48% to 26.84% whereas female literacy varies between 1.65% to 2.89%. These are less urbanised tahsils where Scheduled Caste population is predominantly dependent on agricultural labourers. The tahsils having very low level of literacy are spread over eastern and western Bundelkhand (Fig. 1). Lalitpur (10.07%). Mahroni (9.28%) and Talbehat (7.49%), tahsils of Lalitpur district and Baberu (9.71%), Karwi (7.12%) and Mau (6.67%), tahsils of Banda district stretched in upland area are not well served by the basic facilities of education. Here, very low level of literacy is associated with very low level of urbanization and higher proportion of workers depending on agriculture. The forest cover and undulating topography barring the tahsil of Baberu have hampered the development of infra-structure including roads and educational institutions. Besides, inadequate number of schools, abhorrence of the orthodox, illiterate parents to send their children especially girls to the school and poverty of parents are other causes which still persist in the region. This can be guage out by female literacy which ranges betwean 0.97% to 2.82%.

Spatial Patterns of Male/Female Disparity in Literacy

There are wide disparities in male-female literacy rates both in rural and usban areas. As per 1981 census, the male literacy of Scheduled Caste population of the study region was seven times greater (28.65%) than the female literacy (4.62%). It connotes that Indian society is mainly characterised by male chauvinism; the females are not only degraded but also they are bereft of the right to study (Ramotra, 1988). In fact, India's problem of illiteracy is rooted in female literacy. It is a serious obstacle in limiting the rate of population which is so closely linked with female literacy.

Fig. 2 illustrates very wide sex diversities in literacy rates (ranging between 1.150 to 1.259) in Mahroni, Baberu and Naraini tahsils of the study region. Barring the Jhansi tahsil, the south-west and central part of the study region present the high disparity (ranging between 0.950 to 1.50) in literacy level due to low economic development, backwardness in all respects, severe exploitation and repression of the people both in social and economic terms. Jhansi tahsil has the lowest (0.528) male-female disparity in literacy among the Scheduled Castes and is followed by Orai tahsil (0.642) (Table 1). Both are the District Headquarters having abundant educational institutions, social awakening and agricultural cum industrial centres.

The empirical want of literacy among the Scheduled Caste females is the outcome of long continued economic compulsions forcing the female to take up work to supplement the family resources for making the modest living. They are even engaged in traditional occupational activities, therefore, education is not a functional necessity. It may be pointed out here that the system of early marriage among the Scheduled Castes still prevails in the rural areas, therefore, the girls are not enrolled in schools. Besides, lack of lady teachers and inaccessibility of educational facilities to the girls, poverty of the parents and lack of social rousing are other responsible factors for low level of literacy in the females. In order to promote the educational level and reduce the drop out rates, it is indispensable to identify the basic flaws at the micro level and provide basic infra-structural facilities.

Male/Female Disparity in Urban and Rural Areas

Male-female disparity in urban areas varies from tahsil to tahsil (Fig. 3). With 16.04% of the scheduled castes residing in urban areas, 31.49 per cent persons are literate (Male 46.00%, female 14.59%). Mau (0.242), Orai (0.465) and Jhansi (0.475) tahsils display a low level of disparity index. Orai and Jhansi are the urban centres where educational facilities and social awareness are greater than that of the other centres. Mau tahsil comes in this category due to very small number of Scheduled Caste population residing in Rajapur urban centre only where male urban literacy (10.45%) is 1.70 times greater than female literacy (6.12%). The high disparity (07.40– 0.990) is observed in ten tahsils of the study region namely Baberu (0.967), Mahroni (0.912), Garautha (0.870), Maudaha (0.842), Kulpahar (0.841), Talbehat (0.814), Mauranipur (0.772), Karwi (0.759), Mahoba (0.750) and Charkhari (0.749) which are backward in terms of educational development.

The wide disparity in the literacy rates of male-female among Scheduled Caste persons is striking in rural areas where female literacy rate is astonishingly low (2.70%) in compasison to the male literacy (25.36%) in the study region. In rural India the preference is given to the male child for education over that of female whose duty is confined to the household chores, therefore, enormous female illiteracy is the product of historical, social and economic factors (Chandna and Sindhu, 1980, 98). The lowest disparity (0.802) is noticed in Orai tahsil whereas the Mau tahsil records the highest disparity (1.376) in the literacy rates of male-female in rural areas (Table 1). High (1.150 to 1.300) to very high (1.300 and above) disparity categories cover the all tahsils of Banda and Lalitpur districts and Rath, Charkhari, and Mahoba tahsils of Hamirpur district whereas low (0.850 to 1.000) to very low (∠0.850) disparity is noticed in all the tahsils of Jalaun district and Jhansi and Hamirpur tahsils (Fig. 4).

Disparity Between Non-Scheduled Castes and Scheduled Castes Literacy Rates

The Scheduled Castes population constitutes 25.60% of the Bundelkhand's total population. The average literacy among the Scheduled Caste persons (17.63%) is much lower than non-Scheduled Caste population (32.82%) but higher than the State's Scheduled Caste's literacy rate (14.96%). The Scheduled Castes literacy rate varies from 6.67% (lowest) in Mau tahsil to 31.80% (highest) in Orai tahsil whereas the literacy among the non-Scheduled Castes fluctuates from 20.83% in Mahroni (lowest) to 48.89% in Jhansi (highest) tahsils. The high disparity index (0.500 and above) is noticed in Mau (0.625), Karwi (0.602) and Lalitpur (0.551) tahsils whereas the low disparity sign (0.200-0.350) is marked in all the tahsils of Jalaun and Jhansi districts and Hamirpur, Rath, Maudaha (Hamirpur district) and Naraini tahsil (Banda district (Fig. 5).

The tahsils having irrigational facilities particularly Bundelkhand plain where Scheduled Caste people are associated with agricultural activities both as cultivators and labourers, the literacy rates are high due to social awakening and better educational facilities, therefore, the disparity is low. The tahsils of high and moderate disparity are marked for undulating topography and drought conditions. In these conditions the struggle for living from farming under drought conditions is really very tough, therefore, augmentation of literacy and education among the Scheduled Castes under such discordant conditions has been an extremely slow process. The prevalence of child marriage also affects the female literacy, therefore, there is a practical absence of literacy among the rural females belonging to Scheduled Castes. The wide spacing of the settlements in the Bundelkhand table land still wider spacing of educational institutions in these drought prone areas make it difficult for children to in for education. Poverty and feudal background in the study region are also at the root of educational backwardness of the Scheduled Castes. The study reveals that literacy rate of Scheduled Caste population in all thetahsils is lower than its counterpart of non-Scheduled Castes population literacy rate.

Conclusion

The literacy rates of the region can be determined by historical, social and economic factors. The Scheduled Caste population of the study region is mostly backward in all respects. Their miserable social conditions and pitiable economic conditions make them less inclined to avail the facilities of the education. Consequently they have to depend on agriculture in the form of agricultural labourers. This ts why the level of literacy among the Scheduled Castes in Bundelkhand region is comparatively lower than several other regions. It is in the Bundelkhand low land region that comparatively higher literacy rates have been observed which have seemed to emerge from a sense of social awakening among the Scheduled Castes.

The above study concludes that—

(*i*) The Bundelkhand table land (eastern and south Western parts) which includes the districts of Banda and Lalitpur are backward in terms of Scheduled Caste literacy rate, therefore, the disparity between Scheduled Caste population literacy is very acute and startling.

(*ii*) It is observed that the very high sex disparity index among the Scheduled Castes is the outcome low female literacy in comparison to the male literacy and (*iii*) It is noteworthy here, that illiteracy among females in rural areas is highly alarming.

Generally, it is observed that male-female literacy in ubran areas is higher in comparison to rural areas. It is, therefore, suggested that in order to reduce such alarming inter-tahsil, community and sex disparities, the priority should be given to educate the down-trodden people of the society, especially the females. The Government and the educationists must precipitate the process of educational progress among the Scheduled Castes to display the higher levels of educational achievements.

TABLE 1

Disparity in Literacy

Tahsils	Literacy Rate in SC			Disparity in male-female literacy	Disparity in rural male-female literacy	Disparity in urban male female literacy	Disparity in non-scheduled castes Scheduled Castes literacy
	P	M	F				
1	2	3	4	5	6	7	8
Jalaun	25.56	40.45	7.40	0.819	0.867	0.589	0.242
Konch	27.21	44.39	7.17	0.885	0.919	0.725	0.217
Orai	31.80	47.06	13.10	0.642	0.802	0.465	0.207
Kalpi	17.99	29.38	4.48	0.875	0.915	0.614	0.269
Moth	23.95	39.82	5.15	0.973	1.032	0.739	0.232
Garauntha	20.69	34.90	4.03	1.012	1.042	0.870	0.297
Mauranipur	21.02	35.42	4.64	0.957	1.081	0.772	0.232
Jhansi	31.38	44.48	15.25	0.538	0.972	0.475	0.240

1	2	3	4	5	6	7	8
Talbehat	7.49	13.09	1.16	1.100	1.162	0.814	0.486
Lalitpur	10.07	16.60	2.82	0.801	1.253	0.516	0.551
Mahroni	9.28	16.44	1.03	1.234	1.249	0.912	0.378
Hamirpur	18.45	30.14	4.65	0.872	0.965	0.726	0.279
Rath	15.62	25.61	2.89	1.000	1.158	0.729	0.331
Kulpahar	11.97	20.48	2.12	1.027	1.052	0.841	0.374
Charkhari	14.00	23.83	2.82	0.976	1.206	0.749	0.369
Maudaha	15.31	26.21	2.45	1.085	1.135	0.842	0.338
Mahoba	12.73	21.57	2.63	0.947	1.172	0.750	0.412
Banda	15.68	26.84	2.88	1.025	1.185	0.631	0.371
Baberu	9.71	16.58	0.99	1.259	1.303	0.967	0 414
Naraini	12.85	22.55	1.65	1.183	1.323	0.739	0.336
Karwi	7.12	12.61	1.11	1.081	1.169	0.759	0.602
Mau	6.67	11.73	0.97	1.106	1.376	0.242	0.625
Bundelkhand Region.	17.63	28.65	4.62	0.849	1.025	0.579	0 307

References

1. Govt. of India. *Census of India, Series 22, Part II-B*, Uttar Pradesh.

2. Chandna, R.C. and Sidhu, M.S. (1980) *Introduction of Population Geography*, Kalyani Publishers, New Delhi, p. 98.

3. Kundu, A. and Rao, J.M. (1983). *In equity in Educational Development* : Issues in Measurement, changing structure and its Socio-economic Correlates with Special Reference to India, p 9, Quoted by Ramotra, K.C. (1988) in Scheduled Caste literacy in North-Western India ; A Spatial Perspective, National Geographer, Vol. XXIII, No. 2, P. 148.

4. Ramotra, K.C. (1988). *Scheduled Caste Literacy in North-Western India* : A Spatial Perspective, National Geographer, Vol. XXIII, No. 2, pp. 147-155.

5. Sopher, David, E. (1974). *A Measure of Disparitv*, The Professional Geographer, Vol. 26, No. 4 pp. 389-80 Quoted by Ramotra, K.C. op. cit. p. 148.

6. Sopher, David, E. (1979). *Temporal Disparity as Measure of change*, Professional Geographer, Vol. 31, No. 4, p. 381. Quoted by Ramotra, K.C. op. cit. p. 148.

FOUR

Areal Profiles of Scheduled Caste Concentration in the Economic Sectors of Uttar Pradesh

Dr. Surendra Singh

Introduction

Under Article 341 and 342 of the Indian Constitution under notification No. SRO—2477A, dated 29th October 1956—Government of India, Ministry of Home Affairs, the Sixty four castes that are economically and socially deprived have been scheduled and notified in the entire state of Uttar Pradesh. Besides, two more castes, namely, *Koris* and *Gonds* have also been scheduled for some areas of the state. According to census figures, the total population of Scheduled Castes and Tribes of the state was 185.5 lakh that was 21.0 per cent of the total population of the state in 1971 which had been marginally increased by 0.43 per cent during 1970s, while the corresponding ratio for the country was only 16.12 per cent. This decadal increase in the percentage of Scheduled Castes and Scheduled Tribes (hereafter SC & ST) population may be due to higher natural growth than the growth of the total population. The population strength of SC indicates that the *Chamars* or *Jatavas*,

Pases, Dhobes, Kores and *Balmikes* are the dominating castes that account for nearly 83.51 percent of the total SC & ST population, while ST population is negligible in the state. It is noticeable that the *Chamars* have the highest proportion (54.6%) of the total SC & ST population. In the social perspective, it can be observed that the literacy level among SC & ST population is lower (10.2%) than the total population (21.7%) in 1971, while it was very low (only 7.1%) in 1961. On the other hand, in 1971, nearly one-third share of total SC & ST population (33.76%) was engaged in economic activities. While the corresponding percentage is lower (30.94%) in the structure of the total population.

Multi-dimensional views and various schemes of the Government can be quoted here for the upliftment of the weaker sections of the society particularly of the SC & ST problems. It is being observed now that the socio-economic structure of the SC & ST population is gradually improving. However, they are no doubt, facing the problems of the low levels of literacy, higher dependency ratio in the demorgaphic structure etc. On the other hand, it is fact that they account for higher percentage of the working group (33.8%) than the percentage of the employment of total population (30.9%) particularly in the economy of the entire Uttar Pradesh. Therefore, there must be a comparative study in which it is to be analysed how geographically the distributional patterns of the SC workers in the various sectors of the economy are different and varied from the distributional patterns of the workers of total population. In this connection, the present paper focusses attention on two important distributional aspects of SC population and its solution. These aspects are related to the following aim and objectives of the study as :

(*a*) to elaborate about the general trends of the distribution of SC population in various economic sectors, and

(b) to locate the real trends of SC concentration in the vari ous sectors of the cconomy of Uttar Pradesh.

Methodology

It is necessary to highlight here that the variations and inter-relationships of the areal patterns of SC population is the fundamental task of the present research to analyse sector-wise areal concentration of SC population is also another important aspect. The following statistical measures can be helpful for analysing the distributive phenomena.

1. Measurements of Areal Veriations and Inter-relations

Standard deviation (S.D.) is the absolute measurement of the variability. By calculating mean and standard deviation (S.D.) of the concerned data of SC population, the co-efficient of variation (Co-efficient of variation (C.V.)=(S.D./mean), if one requires the C.V. in percent, multiply it by 100), that is the relative scale of areal variation has been measured for each of the sector of the economy of Uttar Pradesh. Further, the degree of relatedness of the dispersion for the same data has been measured by applying Kart the Pearson method of correlation, r. The concentration is related to the measurement of variability, but it has different meaning and concept of the distribution. It is associated with the density of the distribution which indicates that the density of a particular quantity is being scored in a few areal units. In this connection, the following criterion has been adopted for the concentration of SC population.

2. The Concentration Index

Reviewing the concerned literature, it is noticeable that the concentration measurements have been applied in various fields of social science researches. First, Gini (1909) proposed the 'Index of concentration' by which the extent of a quantity which is concentrated in a few units can be measured.[1] Gini index is the mean-based single dimensional statistical technique which has also been used by Marshal for the measurement of concentration of the functions and functional classification of Canadian cities.[2] It is modified later on by changing its coefficient by Formby and Seaks.[3] Similarly, the Lorangean curve of concentration shows the cumulative scores of distribution on the graph. Note here that both are the absolute measurements of concentration. It has earlier been discussed that the concentration of the phenomena is related to the nature of its density patterns. Thus, the degree of concentration can be calculated by describing the tendencies of distribution. Therefore, 'trend-surface analysis' is also important tool for the same. For distinguishing the areal units of the distributive phenomena, the simple equation of regression model can be applied. The deviations of the actual tendencies of the distribution from hypothetical one can be calculated by finding out the differences occuring in their parameteric changes. On the basis of these changes, the areal units can easily be classified.

The nature of straight line* of the hypothetical trend will be the diagonal line of the graph. It will start from origin of the graph, and its tendency of change will always be at 45° where first order differentiation of this straight line equation will equal to one (b=1.00). While the constant b of the actual distribution will vary according to the nature of the distribution. It is assumed that the SC working population in the various sectors of the economy of the state is inter-related to the total working force in a positive manner, it means that the higher percentage of SC working population is due to the higher percentage of the total working force engaged in the economic sectors of the state, then the SC working (Y coordinate of the graph) will be dependent and vary according to the

* Note that simple equation of straight line is $Y=a+bX$, where a and b are constants and b is related to the rate of change in the distribution.

total work force (X coordinate of the graph) of the various sectors of the economy. Now, it is obvious that the rate of change of SC working population per unit of change of the total work force (dY/dX), i.e., constant as b in the straight line equation will indicate the 'Occupancy rate' of the SC workers employing in the various sectors of economy. If b is higher, the occupancy of SC workers will be greater in the economic sectors and *vice-versa*. Now, the areal distribution of SC workers concentration can be described by classifying total areal units into three categories according to the nature and tendencies of the distribution. They are as the areas of :

(a) *High Concentration*—where the areal units have their positions above the actual regression line on dispersion diagram if $b > 1.00$ and, in case, $b < 1.00$, then the areal units falling above the hypothetical line will be considered as the areal units of high concentration;

(b) *Marginal Concentration*—where the areal units have their positions between the actual and the hypothetical lines; and

(c) *No Concentration* – the rest of the areal units falling below these lines.

For analysing the results in connection with the concentration of SC workers in the various economic sectors, the district is considered as an areal unit (for the names of the districts of Uttar Pradesh, see Table—1) and the related sector-wise statistics of SC as well as total working force of each of the district have been collected and compiled from various census tables like General Population Tables (Part II A) and Social and Cultural Tables (Part II C (I) of the series—21.

The Results

(A) General Patterns of SC & ST Population

Before discussing the focal theme of the present research, the areal patterns of SC & ST population must be elaborated, so that the general personality of SC & ST population can be carved out. Table 1 shows the percentage of SC & ST population and its decadal changes. It indicates the clear picture of the distribution and concludes that the economically backward areas, viz. (*a*) the central dry zone of Uttar Pradesh (the most of the part of middle Ganga-Ghaghra doab), and (*b*) the Southern rugged topographic plateau consisting of the parts of Bundelkhand and Banghelkhand where prevailing geographical condition are not suitable for economic development, particularly for agriculture, have very high percentage of SC & ST population (above 25.0%). Mirzapur, important part of the same category, is the dominant district in SC & ST population which claims more than one-third share of total population (33.5%). The areas of high percentage of Scheduled Castes (25.0—21.0%) i.e., just above the state average, are marked in the lower parts of the Ganga-Ghaghra *doab* excluding a few districts of eastern border. Two hill-border districts (Uttar Kashi and Pithoragarh) and the three districts, that are situated in the middle Ganga-Yamuna *doab* (Saharanpur, Aligarh and Etawah) are also included in the same class of general distribution. On the other hand, the entire western Uttar Pradesh, the central hill districts (larger parts of Garhwal Himalayas) and the entire Northern Terai belt carry low and very low percentages (below 21.0%) of SC & ST population.

An over all decadal growth in the percentage of SC & ST population of the state during 1970s is not much significant; it is only 0.43 percent from 21.0% to 21.43 percent, may be due to higher natural growth of the SC & ST population. However, there seems the areal variations in the distribution of its changing patterns (Table 1). The areas of the Himalayan foothills (particularly the areas of Garhwal and Kumaon Hill districts) and their adjoining Terai parts of the state have the significant growth of SC & ST population. For example, the districts of Dehradun and Nainital of the Himalayas foothills have very high growth (5 to 10%) during the decade. It is due to high rate of migration and natural growth of SC & ST population. The significant high growth (above average) is also noticeable in the Central parts of the Ganga-Jamuna *doab* and in the Central Ganga valley. It reflects the intra-state migration among SC & ST population from the backward areas of the Central parts of the State to the developing areas where they may get more job opportunities.

It is now important to analyse the employment rate and its areal variations particularly of SC population (because it has much significant dominating share among total SC & ST population) in the various sectors of economy of the State.

(*B*) *Areal Variability and Sectoral Comparison*

The district-wise SC working group data according to the economic activities have been collected from the census occupation tables. It is evident to note here that, according to Census classification of working population, the occupation-wise working force has been divided into nine categories : I to IV categories, fall into primary sector of economy; V a & b are recognised as secondary sector; and categories VI to IX have been included in the tertiary sector (Table 2). The Table 2 shows the comparison and areal dispersion of SC workers in various economic sectors. The concerned results can be summarised in the following manner

(*i*) The total worker's share of SC is larger (33.77%) engaging various economic activities than the share of the total working force (30.94%) in the state. It may be due to the employment of SC child population of 12-18 years age group. Therefore, the problems related to child labour exist in SC population.

(*ii*) In fact, the largest share of SC workers (85.58%) is engaged in the primary activities, particularly in agricultural sector of the economy, in which agricultural labour category is accounting for 42.2 percent, i.e., very high rather than the percentage of the total agricultural labourers, while its degree of areal variability is marginally low. It indicates the uniform distribution of SC agricultural labourers in the state. On the other hand, the percentage of SC cultivators is marginally low (43.42%) rather than the percentage of total cultivators and the SC cultivators are highly dispersed in a few patches, particularly in the areas of hill districts and lower Gomati tracts. Indeed, inspite of tightening the land tenancy laws in the state, the larger share of the SC workers is still existing in the landless labour category in agricultural activities.

(*iii*) As far as industrial as well as tertiary activities are concerned, the percentages of SC workers are lower than the employment of total working force except the construction (Category VI) where SC workers have 0.72 percent (Table 2). It is noted here that the degree of their areal variability is much higher in each of the concerned activities. It indicates the scattered tendencies at the low level of employment in the secondary and tertiary sectors of the State economy. It is because of the employment of unskilled SC workers in the construction and repairs of roads, railways and buildings particularly in the lower Ganga-Jamuna *doab* areas of the State where the processes of urbanisation and industrialisation are being accelearated.

Over all, the foregoing description highlights the salient featurers of its level of employment and the distributional characteristics of the SC working force and concludes that there seems the stagnation conditions of SC working force only in the agricultural labour class. More job opportunities can be given to the SC workers in industrial as well as trade, transport and communication activities although they still have lower level of literacy and high poverty.

(*C*) *Sector-Wise Occupancy Rates*

By determinnig the general trends of SC working population with the help of straight line equation (as already discussed) the occupancy rates (parameter b of the equations) of the SC workers have been calculated for each and every economic sector. The higher occupancy rate than one ($b>1$) indicates the greater employment share of SC workers and *vice-versa.* Table 3 summerises the results of SC employment and its correlationships. It clearly shows that the occupations related to the agricultural activities specially cultivators and agricultural labourers and the construction activities (Category VI) accounts for high occupancy rates of SC workers (more than 1.00) with the highly significant correlations with total working force. The service sectors and the household industrial activities have also moderate rates of SC occupancy though its values are marginally lower than the hypothetical one. While the coefficient of corelation between the SC and total working population is low (+.51) and insignificant specially in the industrial sectors of the economy. It indicates that, without co-associating the areal structure of SC workers with total working force, they have been engaged in industrial activities, mostly in those areas where these activities are being developed.

(*D*) *Areal Patterns of SC Workers Concentration*

In fact, the occupancy rate of SC workers has been considered the basic criterion for the classification of areal units in the present study and, therefore, areal patterns of concentration will be influenced by the straight line equations as given in Table 3. According to the criteria of the classification of areal units described logically in the preceding part of the present paper, the districts of Uttar Pradesh have been grouped into three areal categories, namely, the areas of high, marginal and no concentration. The general patterns of concentration of first two categories have been considered here because of the third areal category is not significant for the present purpose.

The sector-wise degree of concentration, the numbers and names of the districts falling into each category have been given in Table 4. It shows the concentration patters of SC working population in detail. On the basis of given table figures, the following patterns of concentration can be generalised.

(*i*) *The Areas of High Concentration* : It has already been noticed that SC workers have the higher occupancy rates in agriculture sector of the economy of the State. With the result, the SC workers particularly engaged in agricultural activities farming as well as landless agricultural labour) have high concentration over the larger parts of the state. It is interesting to note that the areas of the Garhwal and Kumaon hills and the larger parts of the Ganga-Yamuna *doab*, where the percentage of SC population is lower than the state average, have very high degree of concentration. The areas of the eastern parts of the state also have high concentration but it is due to high percentage of SC population. The hill areas and the lower parts of the Ramganga valley have high concentration of farming communities of SC workers. The SC workers' concentration in the industrial activities (that includes household as well as manufacturing industries) is marked high in the Garhwal hill areas, Upper parts of the Ganga-Yamuna *doab* and the entire part of Bundelkhand. While, only the Central parts of the Ganga-Yamuna *doab* is noticeable for high concentration of SC workers' specially in tertiary sectors of the economy.

Now, it can easily be concluded that the areas of hills, entire Gangn-Yamuna *doab* and the Bundelkhand areas of rugged topography are noticeable for high concentration of SC workers engaging in most of the economic activities.

(*ii*) *The Areas of Marginal Concentration* : The areas where rate of occupancy of SC workers is between the actual and hypothetical rates, have been included in this category. Table 4 depicts that the longitudinal belt of the Terai and the entire eastern part of the state are marked as the areas of marginal concentration of SC workers engaging specially in agricultural sectors. The remaining parts of the Bundelkhand and the central plains of the state have also been included in the same category. But these areas have marginal concentration of landless labour occupation. The Kanpur-Lucknow belt of the central plains carries the marginal degree of concentration particularly in the construction activities. Construction of buildings, roads, and railways are improtant activities of this industrial hub area in which SC workers are mostly employed. The SC workers are marginally concentrated in the areas of Terai foothills, partlcularly in trade and commerce activities while the entire part of Rohilkhand is noticeable for transportation and communication activities for the same category of SC workers concentration. An over all picture depicts that the hill areas specially Garhwal region and the Terai belt of Uttar Pradesh are noticeable for marginal concentration of SC working population (Table 4).

Conclusion and Suggestions

Among various measurements of concentration, the relative measurement which is trend-surface based teachique, is also important. The occupancy rates, which have been calculated by fitting straight line equations for SC workers of each economic sector of Uttar Pradesh, are the basic components for classifying the areal units. The areas of no concentration of SC workers may be distinguished for further promotion of the engagement of SC working population. In this connection, a few concrete suggestions may be forwarded for the appropriate and proportionate engagement of SC workers in the economy of Uttar Pradesh. They are as in given below—

(1) The average percentage of SC workers is comparatively higher than the percentage of total workers particularly in the agricultural sector (the categories of cultivators and agricultural labourers i.e., rural dominated sector), while, on the other hand, tertiary sectors of economy

accommodates lower percentages of SC workers. The sectorally balanced economic st ructure of SC workers can be suggested by engaging them in the tertiary sectors where their occupancy rates are low in each of the economic activities.

(2) The primary sect or of economy, excepting Livestock, Forestry, Fishing etc., (Category III), where occupancy rate of SC workers is very low, although the degree of concentration is generally observed throughout the state, should be counter-balanced by providing the employment opportunities specially in the category III of rural allied services.

(3) Both the categories of industrial sector (Va & Vb) carry the low occupancy rates and no concentration of SC workers in the entire eastern parts of Uttar Pradesh including Terai areas. However, the percentage of SC population is higher than the State average. Therefore, under the new industrial development policies, the skilled labour of SC population must be employed particularly in these areas of no concentration.

(4) The Tertiary activities can also absorb more SC workers particularly in the Terai and eastern parts of the State where percentage of SC working population is high with the areas of no concentration, where the eastern parts of Uttar Pradesh have high and/or marginal concentration of most of the activities.

TABLE 1

Percentage of Scheduled Castes and Tribes Population in the Districts of Uttar Pradesh (1971 and 1981)

Sl. No.	*Name of District*	*% of S.C. & S.T. Population* *1971*	*1981*	*Decadal Change (in percentage)*
1	2	3	4	5
1.	Uttar Kashi	23.13	23.10	—0.03
2.	Chamoli	16.77	19.81	+3.04
3.	Tehri Garhwal	13.12	12.83	—0.29
4.	Garhwal	10.57	11.92	+1.35
5.	Pethoragarh	21.24	23.10	+1.86
6.	Almora	19.24	20.92	+1.68
7.	Nainital	17.87	23.00	+5.13
8.	Bijnor	20.26	20.51	+0.25
9.	Moradabad	15.78	17.11	+1.33
10.	Badaun	16.06	16.82	+0.76
11.	Rampur	11.56	13.10	+1.54
12.	Bareilly	11.54	12.54	+1.00
13.	Pilibhit	14.77	17.10	+2.33
14.	Shahajahanpur	16.30	22.13	+5.83
15.	Dehradun	11.65	21.90	+10.25
16.	Saharanpur	23.31	17.81	—5.60
17.	Muzaffernagar	16.54	14.82	—1.72
18.	Meerut	17.80	16.84	—0.96
19.	Bulandshahr	20.54	21.50	+0.96
20,	Aligarh	21.31	22.50	+1.19

Contd,

1	2	3	4	5
21.	Mathura	19.22	19.62	+0.40
22.	Agra	20.75	22.22	+1.47
23.	Etah	16.60	17.10	÷0.50
24.	Mainpuri	17.72	18.43	+0.61
25.	Farrukhabad	17.00	17.42	+0.42
26.	Etawah	24.45	25.41	+0.96
27.	Kanpur	19.76	19.83	+0.07
28.	Fatehpur	23.60	23.71	+0.11
29.	Allahabad	24.68	24.52	—0.16
30.	Jhansi	25.71	28.71	+3.00
31.	Jalaun	27.65	27.22	—0.45
32.	Hamirpur	25.51	24.51	−1.00
33.	Banda	23.07	23.73	+0.65
34.	Kheri	27.05	26.91	—0.14
35.	Sitapur	32.20	31.00	—1.20
36.	Hardoi	31.72	29.92	—0.80
37.	Unnao	29.96	30.21	+0.25
38.	Lucknow	25.06	23.93	—1.13
39.	Rae Bareilly	30.44	29.61	—0.83
40.	Bahraich	17.53	16.82	—0.71
41.	Gonda	17.55	15.80	—1.75
42.	Barabanki	27.92	27.73	—0.20
43.	Faizabad	24.15	24.21	+0.06
44.	Sultanpur	23.90	23.10	—0.80
45.	Pratapgarh	21.23	21.51	+0.28
46.	Basti	20.37	20.00	—0.37
47.	Gorakhpur	21.33	21.51	+0.18
48.	Deoria	15.60	17.42	+1.82
49.	Azamgarh	24,34	24,82	+0.48

1	2	3	4	5
50.	Jaunpur	20.97	21.41	+0.14
51.	Ballia	13.91	15.50	+1.50
52.	Ghazipur	19.37	26.63	+7.26
53.	Varanasi	17.45	18.11	+0.66
54.	Mirzapur	33.58	32.61	—0.97
	Uttar Pradesh	21.00	21.43	+0.43

* Meerut district includes the figures of Ghaziabad and Jhansi district figures are including Lalitpur district for 1981.

Source : Censas of India 1971 and 1981.

TABLE 2

Mean Standard Deviation (S. D.) and Coefficient of Variation (C. V.) in Various Sectors of Economy (1971)

Name of the Categories	*Total Workers*			*Scheduled Castes Workers*		
	Mean (in %)	*S. D.*	*C. V. (in %)*	*Mean (in %)*	*S. D.*	*C. V. (in %)*
1	2	3	4	5	6	7
(A) PRIMARY SECTOR :						
1. Cultivators	57.429	15.242	26.541	43.421	22.560	51.956
2. Agricultral Labourers	19.952	10.520	52.726	42.168	20.620	48.899
3. Livestock, Forestry, Fishing, Hunting and Plantations & other allied activities.	.613	.700	114.192	.572	.570	99.650
4. Mining & Quarrying	.041	—	—	.050	—	—
(B) SECONDARY SECTOR :						
5. Manufacturing, Processing, Servicing & Repairs	7.286	4.200	57.645	4.947	4.071	82.293

1	2	3	4	5	6	7
(C) TERTIARY SECTOR :						
6. Construction	.609	.452	74.220	.718	.781	108.773
7. Trade & Commerce	4.066	2.200	54.107	1.034	1.100	106.383
8. Transport, Storage & Communications	1.733	1.502	86.671	1.103	1.202	108.975
9. Other Services	8.271	5.699	68.901	5.987	5.122	85.552
Total workers	30.942	7.101	22.949	33.766	7.600	22.908

N.B. : 1. The Total Industrial Workers (Category V) have been calculated by combining the working force of both the categories as a V and V b.

2. The Coefficients of variation for category IV are not calculated due to the negligible percentage in the each district of Uttar Pradesh.

TABLE 3

General Trends, Occupany Rates and the Degree of Interrelationships of S. C. Workers for the Various Economic Sectors in Uttar Pradesh (1971)

Name of Economic Sectors	*General Trend* $(Y=bX+a)$*	*Equations*	*Corelation coefficient* (r)
1	2	3	4
Total S.C. Workers	Y= 1.0291	X+ 1.9239	.963020**
(A) AGRICULTURAL SECTOR			
1. Cultivators	Y= 1.4034	X—37.1728	.947408**
2. Agricultural Labourers	Y= 1.8847	X+ 4.5647	.962145**
3. Livestock, Forestry, Fishing, Hunting & Plantations and other allied activities	Y= .6771	X+ .1569	.797935**
(B) INDUSTRIAL SECTOR			
4. Household Industries	Y= .8012	X— .0087	.512318
5. Other than household Industries	Y= .6986	X— .1433	.711886

1	2	3	4
(C) TERTIARY SECTOR			
6. Construction	Y= 1.3230	X— .0877	.791839**
7. Trade & Commerce	Y= .4149	X— .6531	.827615**
8. Transport, Storage & Communication	Y= .7075	X— .1232	.898628**
9. Other Services	Y= .8115	X— .7253	.910029**

N. B. : Due to negligible percentage of Scheduled Castes Workers in the category **IV** of agricultural sector, it is not incorporated in the table.

*In equation, Y=b X+a; where 'a' & 'b' are the perameters of the equation and X and Y are the percentages of total as well as Scheduled Castes' workers respectively.

**The values are significant at .05 level.

TABLE 4

Name of the Districts of Scheduled Castes' Construction by Various Economic Sectors of Uttar Pradesh (1971)

Economic Sectors	*Total No. of distt. having Concentration*	*Seri ıl No. of Districts Under* — *High Concent-rations*	*Marginal Concentration*
1	2	3	4
Total Scheduled Castes' Workers	44	3, 4, 6, 7, 11, 16, 28, 29, 30, 32, 33, 38, 39, 41, 42, 43, 44, 45, 46, 47, 48, 49, 50, 51, 52, 53, 54, (27)	2, 5, 8, 10, 12, 13, 17, 18, 19, 22, 24, 25, 26, 27, 31, 36, 37, (17)
1. Cultivators	26	1, 2, 4, 5, 6, 11, 12, 35, 50. (9)	7, 8, 9, 13, 14, 15, 16, 20, 30, 37, 38, 39, 42, 47, 49, 53, 54. (17)

1	2	3	4
II. Agricultural Labourers	54	15, 16, 18, 19, 20, 21, 22, 26, 27, 28, 31, 34, 35, 36, 39, 41, 42, 43, 44, 45, 46, 48, 49, 50, 53. (25)	Rest all Districts (29)
III. Livestock, Forestry, Fishing, Hunting etc.	14	10, 14, 20, 21, 23, 24, 25, 26, 36. (9)	15, 18, 19, 27, 54. (5)
IV. (a) Household Industries	23	1, 2, 3, 4, 5, 6, 7, 15, 16, 17, 18, 21, 23, 30, 31, 32. (16)	13, 19, 25, 26, 27, 37, 38 (7)
V. (b) Other than Household Induatries	21	2, 3, 4, 5, 6, 17, 22, 24. (8)	1, 7, 18, 27, 32, 33, 39, 40, 48, 49, 50, 51, 52. (13)

Contd.

1	2	3	4
VI. Construction	23	5, 6, 19, 20, 21, 22, 23, 24, 26, 30, 31, 32, 33. (13)	2, 3, 4, 7, 10, 17, 25, 27, 28, 29. (10)
VII. Trade & Commerce	10	———	3, 4, 5, 6, 13, 15, 18, 20, 31, 52, (10)
VIII. Transport, Storage & Communication	24	7, 9, 23, 24, 45, 48. (6)	1, 2, 3, 4, 5, 6, 10, 18, 19, 20, 21, 27, 28, 30, 33, 35, 36, 53. (18)
IX. Other Services	17	19, 20, 21, 22, 23, 24, 25. (7)	29, 33, 40, 41, 42, 43, 44, 45, 46, 47. (10)

N. B. : (1) For the name of districts and the index of their serial Nos, see Table—1.

(2) Category IV of economic activities has not been included in the Table due to negiligible percentage of S. C. workers.

References

1. Kendall, M.G. and W.R. Wuckland : *A Dictionary of Statistical Terms,'* III edition, Oliver & Boyd, Edinburg (1971), p. 28

2. Marshall, John U. : 'City Size, Economic Diversity, and Functional Type : The Canadian Case, '*Economic Geography* Vol. 51, No. 1 (1975), pp. 37-49

3. Formby, John P. & T.G. Seaks : 'Paglin's Gini Measure of Inequality—A Modification' *The American Economic Review*, Vol. 70, No. 3 (1980). pp. 479-82.

FIVE

Women's Age at Marriage its Among Scheduled Castes and Implications: Theoritical and Empirical Explorations

Dr. S.B. Singh Parmar

Introduction

Age, although a physiological variable, has great socio-cultural significance. All societies recognise age as a basis of the social status and divide biological time into social relevant units. "Upon the rich tapestry supplied by the organic age grid societies weave varying social arrangements" (Levingston et. al., 1978 : 57). The cycle of growth from infancy to adulthood creates discontinuities in the life cycle—a fact of nature which is inescapable (Parsons, 1942 : 604-616; Vinake and Wilson, 1964 241-248). While age itself is largely beyond the individual's or society's determination, the attention paid to, and the meaning attached with, it vary considerably between and within societies (Eisenstadt, 1964). "Age graded cultures," says Benedict (1938: 161-168), "Characteristically demand different behaviour of the individual at different times of his life and persons of a likes age grade are grouped into society whose activities are all oriented towards the behaviour desired at that age. Individuals "graduate" publically and with howour from one of these groups to another."

Besides, or so to speak, above these general socio-cultural implications, the age at which women marry assumes special significance and has far reaching implications at both the macro and micro levels. At the macro level, it affects demographic structure of a nation. It is almost a sociological truism that women who marry late tend to procreate fewer children than those who marry early (see, e.g. Chandrashekharan, 1959: 09; Blake, 1967: 132; Bushfield, 1972: 117-134; Chaudhury, 1983: 143; Bhatia, 1983: 189; Parmar, 1986: 106-112). Women's age at marriage, thus, determines not only the ultimate family size but also the population size of that country (Agrawal, 1967: 172; Baldwin, 1977 : 02; United Nations, 1980: 04). At the micro level, the age at which a woman is married and has her first child is of utmost importance in her integration in economic development. The age of a woman when she has her first child has a decisive influence on her studies and, therefore, her possibilities for advancement. Once young girl has a baby, it means that she has to leave school, and consequently later on without a proper education will be unable to find a job and participate in the development process.

Women's Age at Marriage : The Indian Social Scenario

There are several factors that combine in one to encourage women's marriage at an early age. One potential factor for women's early age at marriage is tradition established and supported by sacred texts. In *Dharmasatras* there are several passages to show that the marriage at an early age was desired and acclaimed. She must be married before she has reached the age of puberty and her guardians have not married her even within three monthly periods, she was allowed to contract a marriage on her own. According to some of the writers of the *Grihyasutras*, the marriage of a girl should be solemnized when she is still *Nagnika* through fear of her attaining puberty. In *Manu Samhita*, it is said that a man of thirty marry a girl of twelve and a man of twenty four a girl of eight Likewise, in *Mahabharat*, the ages of husband and wife are said to be thirty and ten or twenty one ond seven. *Vaikhanasa Sutra* mentions that a Brahmin should marry a girl who is *nagnika* (a girl over eight years and below twelve) or *gauri* (between ten and twelve) who has not had her menstruation period. *Bramhacharya* for a girl, according to *Laugaksi Grihyasutra*, lasts till tenth or twelfth year. The Brahmanik literature of the early Christian era ordains that the daughter be married between the ages of ten and twelve. All these (there are many other sources) show that from the time *Dharmasastras* a trend in favour of the early marriage of girls as soon as they attained puberty became conspicuous. Altekar (1973 : 55-56) has pointed out that from about 200 A.D. early marriages became very common throughout India.

The virginity became one of the qualifications for marriage of girls. And, once virginity became virtue and emblem of respectability, it became a sign of the elite and an index of high caste. Hence marriage was desired by the society before she attains puberty. Another contributory factor for the early marriage was the conception of *Samskara*. Vivaha (marriage) *Samskara* is said to be the vedic sacrament for women. A female child was not considered worthy of all the *Samskaras*, and the only *Samskara* to be performed in her case was marriage, else she is no better than a sudra.

Another, a second, contributory factor for an early age marriage of women is the androcentric biases—the male prejudices that women is not fit to remain independent in her life, be a child, young or old—the negation of her personality. When a girl has grown young she must go under the domination and tutelage of her husband and, hence, be married as early as possible. Why should a girl be married at an early age ? The male holds prejudicial view in respect of her sexual appetite. "Women must particularly be guarded against evil inclinations, however trifling they may appear to be : for, if they are not guarded, they will bring sorrow on both the families. Considering it the highest duty of all castes even weak husbands must strive to guard their wives" (Manu, quoted in Kapadia, Marriage and Family in India, pp. 253-254). It is the result of the male biases that girls younger than boys came to be preferred so that she can not question the latter and exercise a controlling voice.

Thirdly, the social ideal of monogamy also contributed to the development towards early marriage. Gradually no, the social prestige came to be attached with early marriage. It was a sign of one's affluence influence and status to get one's child betrothed before she reached the age of puberty and it was a matter of pride and prestige that one's child was sought after a tender age.

Fourthly, the Muslim invaders started snatching Hindu girls forcibly. Consequently, child marriage became the norm of the society.

Finally, for the poor, more hands are needed to ensure their survival. Though it is true for all the poor, it is more true of the Scheduled Castes and Tribes in India for, they are poorest among the poor. Let us substantiate this fact with data. The 32nd round of the National Sample Survey Organisation of 197:-78, which was first of the NSSO survey to separate out Scheduled Castes and Tribes. For the purpose of the exercise, the poverty line was drawn at the figure of Rs. 65 per capita per month in the rural areas and Rs. 75 in urban areas. Of Indians, who fell beneath this poverty line, 18.11 per cent were Scheduled Caste and 9.66 per cent Scheduled Tribe persons. So 27.7 per cent of the poor were Scheduled Caste and Scheduled Tribes, whereas their share of the Indian Population was 21.57

per cent. But once the poverty figure is divided in half, a more dramatic picture emerges. Fully 40.60 per cent of Indians living on less than half the poverty figure are from the Scheduled communities. In other words, the lower you draw your poverty line, the greater the proportion of Scheduled persons you will met. The striving parents, particularly from these communities, often pledge their children as a last desperate measure. The desperate situation induces women to produce more children as their last hope of survival. Children born to the poor are a tangible asset. The poor need more children to supplement the family income. And, the early marriage becomes a must.

Under the influence of these and many other forces, early marriage became more popular and with the passage of time the custom became hardened that a departure from it was a matter of social disapproval and even social disgrace. The lower castes in their imitation of the higher outmarted by contracting marriage even before birth of a child, that is she was in the womb. Karva (1965 : 138) confirms this fact by stating that marriages of the children were settled by the parents even before they were born. The Indian Penal Code of 1860 declared consumation when the wife was below ten years of age safe and prescribed punishment. The Child Marriage Restraint Act was passed in 1929 which laid down that a male under eighteen years and a female under fourteen years was considered a child. The Hindu Marriage Act of 1955 accepts fifteen years as the minimum age at marriage in the case of a girl which has now been raised to 18 years by an amendment of 1978. But there is no need to comment that even this recent legislation is very retrogressive (For more details on age at marriage see Kapadia, 1968 : 138-166).

The preceding review exercise, then, shows that early marriage of girls tends to be the trend of marriage in India.

Forty years removed from independence, it will be interesting to find out the prevailing age at marriage for girls and desired age at marriage by their parents in general among the Scheduled Castes in particular.

Objectives

This inquiry has a two-fold objective : one, to ascertain the recent trends in the age at marriage of women among the Scheduled Castes, and two, to determine the attitude of women towards the age at marriage.

Hypotheses

In the light of traditional socio-cultural matrix and contemporary situation of Indian society our hypotheses are :

1. Women's age at marriage among Scheduled Castes tends to be low.
2. The actual age at which people marry their daughters is likely to be different from the desired age at marriage.

Research Design

The study has an exploratory-cum-descriptive design. While its main purpose is to make an exploratory study of the women's age at marriage, it proposes to test certain hypotheses which have been formulated on thc basis of the conditions prevailing in the Indian Society and also with the help of available research material.

Data Sources

The data for the present study was collected in between August and October, 1983 from married women of village 'Mangawan' in the Manikpur block of the Banda district, Uttar Pradesh. Nearly 84 per cent habitants of this village belong to the Scheduled Castes. The village is located 25 Kms. West of Manikpur. It can be approached either by train or by muddy forest track via 'Markundi'. The Railway Station

'Tikaria' is situated in the village itself. Out of 168 married women, 100 were selected by systematic random sampling procedure for proper investigation and analysis.

The data was collected with help of interview schedule specially constructed for the above purpose. In order to supplement the quantitative data, qualitative data was collected by observation during the course of interview.

Social Characteristics of the Respondents :

The table 1 shows that all the women interviewed totally illiterate. Majority of them were engaged in agricultural related

TABLE 1

Social Characteristics of the Respondents, in Percent.

Social Characteristics	*Percent*
Education	
Illiterate	100
Primary Education	—
Secondary and Higher Education	—
Occupation of Husbands	
Agriculture	98
Others	02
Age Group	
15—24	20
25—34	39
35—44	41
Number of cases	100

occupations. About 30 per cent of the holdings in the village, belong to Scheduled Castes but majority of them serve as agricultural labourers. Coming to the age structure of the respondents, 20 per cent of them were in the age group 15-24 years and another 39 per cent in the age group 25-34 years, whereas the remaining 41 per cent were in the age group 35-44 years. Average age of the respondents was 32.1 years.

Analysis and Discussion

Women's Age at Marriage :

Women's age at marriage can be viewed from two angles—actual and effective. Actual age refers to the age at which girls are married. However, most wide spread custom is that girls are married but in all the cases they do not join their husbands immediately after marriage. The girls are married at an early age but join their husbands by a second ceremony a few years later. The age at this second ceremony is more important because it is the beginning of actual married life. Hence, this has been termed as effective age at marriage in this study. Where the girls join their husbands soon after marriage, actual and effective ages are the same there.

Table 2 presents actual (when married) and effective (when joined their husbands) age at marriage.

As is evident from table 2, the trend of early marriage is prevalent among the women of Scheduled Castes. In so far as the actual age at marriage is concerned, 94 per cent women were married between 5 and 19 years of age and only 6 per cent at the age of 20 years and above. The break up of the percentage of those married at age group 5-19 years reveals that 7 per cent girls were married in between 5 and 9 years, 71 per cent in between 10 and 14 years and 16 per cent in between 15 and 19 years. The mean of actual age at marriage comes to 13.0 years.

TABLE 2

Women's Actual and Effective Age at Marriage, in Percent

Age at Marriage	*Women in percent*
Actual Age at Marriage	
5—9 years	07
10—14 years	71
15—19 years	16
20—24 years	06
Effective Age at Marriage	
10—14 years	35
15--19 years	56
20—24 years	09
Number of Cases	100

Mean age at marriage—

1. Actual 13.0 years
2. Effective 15.7 years

The Table makes it obvious that the effective age at marriage, too, is very low among Scheduled Castes. 91 per cent women joined their husbands in the early years of their reproductive span and only 9 per cent at the age of 0 years and above. Of 91 per cent who joined their husbands at an early age, 35 per cent joined in between 10—14 years and 56 per cent in between 15—19 years of age. The mean of effective age at marriage comes to 15.7 years. This then shows that the age at marriage among the women of Scheduled Castes is still very low. And, this confirms our hypothesis that no drastic shift in the age at marriage is likely to occur in view of hard crust of tradition.

Future Trends in Age at Marriage :

While relating opinions regarding suitable age at marriage to actual age at which they married their daughters, it was found that desired age at marriage was higher than the actual age. Table 3 presents the distribution of respondents by their preferred age at marriage and the age at which they actually married their daughters.

TABLE 3

Distribution of Respondents by their Desired Age at Marrige and Daughter's Actual Age at Marriage, in Percent

Age in Years	*Desired Age Marriage*	*Actual Age at Marriage*
5—9	—	07
10—14	72	71
15—19	27	16
20—24	01	06
Number of Cases	(100)	(100)
Mean age at marriage	13.5 years	13.0 years

A look at table 3 makes it obvious that the women do not prefer at all to marry their daughters in the low age group of 5-9 years but in actual practice they do so. Similarly they do not favour late marriages too, as only one per cent women preferred to marry their daughters at the age of 20 years and above, whereas in actual practice 6 per cent did so. The table further reveals that 99 per cent women prefer to marry their daughters in between 10-19 years age group. Of these, 72 per cent favoured 10-14 years age group while 27 per cent preferred 15-19 years age group. It is interesting to note that an upward trend in the age at marriage hat been noticed but late marriages, too, are not considered proper. In actual practice, the late marriages (20 years and above) have been performed due to adverse family circumstances, as it was stated by the respondents during investigations. The girl's age at marriage, considered most suitable, was in between 10-19 years.

A Pause

The implication of early age at marriage for the Scheduled Caste women are varied. They are married early, and hence, they are likely to become mothers relatively early. Early motherhood, in turn, weakens the health, increases the chances of female mortality, and burdens the task of child rearing. Since these women come from poor families they had to work for their survival when in their family way as also after delivery. They also lack nutrition. All this conjointly tells upon the health of the women. The girls who are married early have their education and for want of adequate education, their entry to the suitable jobs is blocked. This blocks not only their career but it also deprives them from participation in development.

Plagued with poverty, weakened by reproduction process, retarded in education, these women become dependent on their family members and remain subject to exploitation. The and rocentric biases, social customs and personal conditions work severally and conjointly against Scheduled Caste women. All this has serious repercussions for women themselves and society at large.

Conclusions

In what has gone before an attempt was made to find out women's age at marriage as in practice among Scheduled Castes as also the desired age at marriage by the women for their daughters. The major conclusionts of the study are as follows :

1. The girls among the Scheduled Castes in village India are married relatively at an early age, generally before, may much before, attaining the statutory age of 18 years.
2. The Scheduled Caste women preferred to marry their daughters at a later age and, thus, they are opposed to the actual age at marriage. Although, a rising trend in the age at marriage seems to be in offing but it is not much encouraging because women do not prefer marriages, too late, for their daughters.

This lend credence to our hypotheses that women's age at marriage among Scheduled Castes tends to show a rising trend and the actual age at which people marry their daughters is different than the desired age at marriage.

These findings have far reaching implications as regards the position of Scheduled Caste Women in the Indian society. Early age at marriage is mainly responsible for their subordinate position and male dominance which adversely affects the development of the society.

Acknowledgement

The author is indebted to Dr. Rajendra Pandey, Professor of Sociology, Department of Humanities and Social Sciences, Indian Institute of Technology, Kanpur for his critical readings, modifications and helpful suggestions.

References

Agrawal, S.N. 1967, Effect of a rise in female age on birth rates in India, *Proceedings of the World Population Conference 1965*, New York: United Nations.

Altekar, A.S. 1973, *The Position of Women in Hindu Civilization* Delhi : Motilal Banarasi Das.

Baldwin, Stephen, 1977, *Nuptiality and Population Policy : An Investigation in Tunisia, Srilanka and Malayasia*, New York : The Population Council.

Benedict, Ruth, 1938, "Continuities and Discontinuities in Cultural Conditioning, *Psychistry*, Vol. 1.

Blake, Judith, 1967, Parental control, delayed marriage and population policy, *Proceedings of the World Population Conference, 1965*. New York: United Nations.

Bhatia, J. C., 1983, Age at Marriage and Fertility in Ghana (West Africa), *Demography India*, Vol. 12, No. 2.

Busfield, John, 1972, Age at Marriage as a variable in socio-economic differentials in Fertility, *Demography*, 6 (1).

Chandrashekharan, S., 1959, *Indian Population Problem*, paper presented at the inaugural conference of United Nations Demographic Teaching and Research Centre, Bombay, Nov.

Chaudhury, R. N., 1983, The influence of female education, labour force participation and age at marriage on fertility behaviour in Bangla Desh, *Janasamkhya*, Vol. 1, No. 2.

Eisenstadt, S.N., 1964, *From Generation to Generation*, New York : The Free Press.

Kapdia, K.M., 1968, *Marriage and Family in India*, Calcutta, Oxford Universty Press.

Karva, I, 1965, *Kinship Organisation in India*, Bombay : Asia Publishing House.

Levington, Daniel J. et. al. 1978 *The Seasons of Man's Life*, New York, Alfred A Knoof.

Parmar, S.B. Singh, 1986, Striyon Men Vivah Ki Ayu Tatha Prajanan Dar Nirdharan : Kol Janajati Par Adharit Ek Addhayan, *Manava*, Vol. 14, No. 2 and 3.

Parsons, Talcott, 1942, Age and Sex in the Social Structure of the United States, *American Sociological Review*, 7 (October) : 604-616.

United Nations Population Divisou Report 1980, *Some Factors Affecting in Fertility Eight Developing Countries.*

Vinacke, W.E., and W.R. Wilson (eds), 1964, *Dimensions of Social Psychology*, Bombay, D.B. Taraporevala Sons and Co.

SIX

Changing the Status of the Scheduled Castes

Dr. R.L. Maurya

Change in the status of the Scheduled Castes involves ameliorative change. The assumption that social phenomena are interconnected and that change in a given set of social phenomena is the result of change in the related sets of phenomena (D' souza, 1981 : 2) implies that change in the status of the Scheduled Castes is contingent upon solution of the age-old social problems permeating in the contemporary society and that led them down. It presupposes change in a set of social phenomena related to their social position considered responsible for the problematic state of the status of the Scheduled Castes. On the other hand, the idea of "changing" the status of the Scheduled Castes involves deliberate action directed towards that end. It is, therefore, pertinent to regard the problem in proper perspectives.

Status Syndrome and Ranking of Statuses

Status means social standing on the basis of which the individuals are ranked higher or lower or at the same level in relation to others (Rose and Rose, 1969 : 321). According to

Parkin, "Status can be regarded as one example of an important non-material reward which is unequally distributed (Parkin, 1971 : 3). Broadly speaking, status refers to the position of the individuals and groups in the society, which is unequally distributed depending on certain differences. Different statuses carry unequally distributed rights, privileges, opportunities, advantages, powers, prestige and monetary rewards associated there with.

Ranking of statuses is the outcome of the system of stratification. In the system of social stratification the "society is conceptually divided into several classes forming a status hierarchy" (Rose and Rose, 1969 : 595). On the other hand, in the status hierarchy "individuals and groups are rated higher than others and with such differences in rating go differences in opportunities and privilages" (Ogburn and Nimkoff, 1964:345). As stated by Ross, "Statuses are ranked, some being considered higher than others. The rank of a status is variously expressed in prestige, power or monetary reward" (Ross, 1963:179). Besides it, "a specific style of life can be expected from all those who wish to belong to the circle. Linked with this expectation are restrictions on 'social intercourse...." (Gerth and Mills, 1967 : 187).

Social stratification and ranking of statuses on the basis of social inequalities, is a universal phenomenon. On the other hand, social inequalities are ubiquitous phenomena depending on the basis and the criteria of social stratification and ranking of statuses. Differential bases and criteria of social stratification and ranking of statuses create social inequalities. Although social inequalities are ubiquitous "the problems stemming from them are not the same everywhere. One of the reasons for this difference is the variation in the form and content of social inequalities" (D' souza, 1981:18).

On the basis of the criteria of social stratification and ranking of the statuses, social inequalities may be classified into two major categories. First, the social inequalities that are universal and ubiquitous and which are unavoidable and are universally accepted. It includes even unamendable social inequalities. Secondly, the social inequalities that are unequally determined on the basis of differential criteria relating to ethnicity and the idea of purity or impurity of occupations and which are limited to a given society, as, for example, social inequalities based on caste system in India. Social inequalities of second type create undesirable and destructive conditions and therefore can be regarded as a social problem. It can be checked.

Retrospection of the Status of the Scheduled Castes

The life that the Scheduled Castes have lived for centuries in the past, has been miscrable. The aggrieved state of life of these people emerged due to their unequal placement in the system of social stratification which not only led to unequal distribution of statuses ascribable through birth but also implied inequality of distribution of rights, privileges, opportunities, power, prestige, monetary reward, etc. on the one hand, and imposition of disabilities on these castes resulting in their deprivation of rights, privileges, opportunities, power, prestige, monetary rewards, etc., on the other. The disabilities imposed upon them got institutionalized as the precepts and directives of the caste system which was supported by the theological and religious philosophy of Hinduism. The institutionalization of the disabilities and thereby deprivation of equality of status made them suffer all the pains forced upon them. It was a result of social inequality inflicted upon them long age in the antiquity.

Since the problem of change in the status of the Scheduled Castes emanated from the problem of social inequality perpetuated traditionally, it is necessary to survey the traditional perspectives of the status of these people so that the problematic dimensions under consideration could be delineated.

The status of the Scheduled Castes is viewed in relation to the other groups of castes taken together in the frame-work of caste system in which all the obligations and barriers are entailed (Gerth and Mills, 1967 : 405) and in which ethnic groups as a corporate whole are placed higher or lower than one another (Marriott, 1961 : 32). The caste system, as viewed by Ghurye,

(i) divides the society into segments and reates social distance between different castes;

(ii) rank Caste-groups hierarchically;

(iii) restricts feeding and social intercourse;

(iv) prescribes civil and religious disabilities and privileges;

(v) restricts choice of occupation, and

(vi) restricts inter-caste marriage (Ghurye, 1969 : 2-20).

It means that the caste system largely determines the social inequalities, the status, available opportunities as well as the handicaps of different caste-groups. Therefore, as expressed by Mehta and Patel, "One of the greatest drawbacks in our social structure is the existence of the caste system dividing the society according to status and rank. Whatever might have been the origin of the caste system, it has given rise to various gradations in the society which, in its turn, has resulted in social inequality and discrimination" (Mehta and Patel, 1995 : 21). Since the status of a caste or caste-group "is based on ritual interaction and is indirectly influenced by economic, political and other non-ritual hierarchies of interactions (Marriott, 1968 : 43), "there is a close correlation between the position of caste in the hierarchy of the Hindu social order and the respective status of its members with regard to wealth, economic rank, class position, political power and accessibility to education and culture" (Desai, 1959 ; 121-122).

In the caste system the status of the caste is fixed and is ascribed through birth. On the other hand, the caste system attaches inherited inequalities as a guiding principle in social relationships (Davis, 1967 : 337). In the status hierarchy of the castes, the Scheduled Castes are placed in the bottom. It is believed that this inequalitarian system of social stratification was based on the idea of purity, whether ritual or occupational. Since the Scheduled castes were considered impure both ritually and occupationally, they were degraded to represent the inferior most group of castes. On account of the idea of ritual impurity based on their unclean occupations, they were degraded to the position of untouchable and unapproachable and were excluded from Hindu rites and rituals. For, as Stated by Mayer, "Because each caste is said to have some link between its occupation and divine decisions and actions, occupation is not only traditionally but also religiously linked with castes" (Mayer, 1965 : 61-62).

Degradation of these castes led to imposition of disabilities in all the social, ritual, economic and political matters. Besides it, degradation of these castes also led to economic, educational and political deprivation on the one hand and to oppression and exploitation on the other. This is evident from the fact that in the past they had no assets; they had to serve as serfs and servants; they had to survive on whatever the dominant castes provided. Such expression are contained in the writings of the Dharmashastra writers who commanded the whole society in almost all the matters—social, economic, religious, political etc. Manu imposing servility on the inferior castes (shudras) declared that the God Himself commanded that it was the duty of the shudras to serve the higher castes without grude (Manusmriti, I : 91). On the other hand, Manu declaring that nothing belongs to the shudras as his own, advised the higher castes to dispossess them of wealth and property (see, Manusmiriti, X. 129). Manu also advised the higher castes to not let them be free even in respect of their own food, clothes, shelters etc., but to allow them to live on the leavings food, the old clothes and the old furnitures of the higher castes (Manusmiriti, X. 125). Thus, the Scheduled Castes holding a servile position in the tradit ional society "had been a down-trodden people. There was a time when they lived poor life, possessed no wealth or property, had no proper dwelling or even a shelter to save themselves from sun and rain. Apart from this, they were exploited by the higher castes at their will. Their poverty and want of economic independence kept them in degraded position" (Report of D. Cs and A. Ts. C., 1930 : 39). Moreover, no noble and profilic occupations were allowed to them and, therefore, they had to live by working in the occupations like leather work, weaving, fishing, hunting and other unclean works (Macdonell and Keith, 1968 : 255-267). Thus, they held lowest position in the economic sphere (Sharma, 1958:54).

The fact that different occupations are graded higher or lower and are considered ritually as clean or unclean and that the Scheduled Castes followed occupations of lowest prestige consisting of menial and unclean works has placed them in the lowest position in the social hierarchy of castes.

Education has always been recognized as a prestigious achievement and as an instrument in improving social and economic conditions. In the traditional Indian society, it was an exclusive preserve of the privileged section of castes and, the people now termed as the Scheduled Castes, had no chance to get education. The idea of the Ashram system exemplifies the exclusion and deprivation of these people from education in the educational scheme of the traditional caste-oriented society. It means that in the traditional Indian society they lacked education due to non-accessibility to it. This state of affairs continued until the then British Government declared a policy of uniform access to educational institutions in the nineteenth century. Otherwise, even "in the pre-British and early British days no attempt was made to educate the Depressed Classes, education being confined to the higher classes" (Ghurye, 1969 : 275-276); Hutton, 1951 : 200-201). Nevertheless, as put in a Report of the Commissioner for Scheduled Castes and Scheduled Tribes, they could not progress in education partly because of the strong caste prejudices and practice of untouchability (1981-82:60).

Problematic Dimensions for Change

The traditional perspectives of the status of the Scheduled Castes, presented in brief as above, make it obvious that the problem of degradation of the Scheduled Castes emerged as a result of social stratification in which status was ascribed through birth and which was institutionalized in the framework of the caste system. In the light of the perspectives presented above, there are different types of problematic issues permeating in the contemporary Indian Society to be tackled for the amelioration of the status of the Scheduled Castes. They may be classified as follows :

(*i*) *Hereditary Inferiority* : They ascribe by birth in a lowest status group of castes and which is the result of traditional social stratification and ranking of statuses and the placement of the Scheduled Castes in a despicable position. "Social stratification and status hierarchy are the warp and woof of social structure and social organization; as such, they are unavoidable in a complex society, although they are modifiable" (D'souza, 1981 : 43).

(*ii*) *Lowest Prestige Occupation alongwith Disabilities and Deprivation* : They inherit as a low caste from generation to generation. As stated by D'souza, "Occupational prestige has been taken to be the major empirical referent and indicator of social inequalities. Therefore, inequality of occupational prestige is the most significant kind of social inequalities. Occupations are universally followed in complex societies and one's occupation has an influence on almost every aspect of one's life" (D'souza, 1981 : 43). The propounders of the rules of the caste system declared lowest prestige occupations as the "Dharma" of these castes with the argument that it was a "command" of the God 'Himself' (Manusmiriti, I.91). The Scheduled Castes having no alternative had to obey it. Consequently, they have to follow the hideous and arduous and such other functions which are considered degrading in nature and which the other groups do not like to do. As, for example, tanning, flaying, removing carrion, sweeping and scavenging, pig rearing, washing clothes, bone collection, shoe making, basket making, rope making, weaving, carpentary, ironsmithy, labour work and such other functions which are also degrading in scale are pursued by the Scheduled Castes. Although, they are now free from all kinds of disabilities and deprivation, they are caught up in a vicious circle of degraded occupations which was generated far back in the antiquity. These lowest prestige occupations impede development and upliftment of these people.

(*iii*) *Stigma of Untouchability* : originated on account of the idea of ritual purity and despicability of the occupations followed by the Scheduled Castes, which, in its turn, led to imposition of disabilities upon them and discrimination against them in the ritual and social matters. The stigma of untouchability and thereby imposition of disabilities led to exclusion of these castes from the rites and rituals of the Hindus and from social intercourse. Such exclusion further degraded their social position. Although, untouchability Constitutionaily as well as by law has been abolished, observation of practical life and studies undertaken by scholars indicate that the stigma of untouchability stands as a strong-hold to be broken. In fact, untouchability has become so deeply ingrained in the social behaviour that, ironically, the Scheduled Castes themselves have created social gradations among them, based as they are, on their consideration of low and very low castes and occupations and this untouchability among them is as faithfully practised as by the higher castes Hindus against them as a whole,

(*iv*) *Educational Disparity* : has been a major problem. In the traditional Indian society the Scheduled Castes were handicapped by imposing inaccessability to education mainly for keeping them down and ignorant of the tricks of deprivation of rights and opportunities. Inaccessibility to education stood as a major impediment in the way of their movement from their appointed station in the society. No doubt, now, there is no problem of inaccessability to education. Nevertheless, they lag much behind in education as compared to other sections of society. On the other hand, education is a foremost requirement for raising social status.

(*v*) *Tendency for Perpetuating Inequalities* : has its root in the outlook of the people as a result of social legitimization of the idea of born inequality as divine or nature-ordained. The continuity of the age-old social structure has led to acceptance of its forms as a reality. In fact, the tendency for perpetuating inequalities is inherent in the social structure and social organization in the frame work of the caste system, which has left no choices to the Scheduled Castes but to react or to accept caste subordination in traditional ways. It is a pity that inspite of professed aims of and commitments to raise the Scheduled Castes from their degraded position, the caste Hindus themselves have done little to prove their sincerity. In fact, there numerous instances in the general behavioural pattern which lend ample justification to the view that they may be indirectly seeking to perpetuate this kind of discrimination. This tendency for perpetuation of social inequalities has been one of the greatest drawbacks in keeping the Scheduled Castes degraded. Because "The tendency for the inter-generational perpetuation of social positions represents a major form of oppression and exploitation in society...." (D'souza, 1981 : 43). Nevertheless, "there is no inseparable connection between a social organization and the tendency towards inter-generational perpetuation of social position" (D'souza, 1981 : 43).

Thus, the social inequality between the Scheduled Castes and the other groups of castes is a problem of the traditional

Indian society in which they were put in a destituted position. The problem of low status of the Scheduled Castes emanated from the problem of social inequalities of the traditional Indian social structure generated long-ago in the antiquity in which they have been graded as a inferiormost group of castes alongwith imposition of disabilities in almost all spheres of life.

Change Strategy

To bring about change in the status of the Scheduled Castes, it is necessary to bring about radical changes in certain ruling trends. Through change the Scheduled Castes "have to achieve a status pattern whereby they arrive at the state of normalcy with other caste people so far the status-syndrome is concerned" (Singhi, 1979 : ix). This involves radical social change. Social changes in this context "imply creating condition through such appropriate means whereby these people do not continue to remain deprived due to iheir status-ascription nor due to any institutionalized disabilities. These groups ought to become so diffused in the professional, vocational, educational, social and other relevant areas of life that they become part of the normalcy of the social stratification and groups therein without stigma and institutionalized deprivation" (Singhi, 1979 : ix). In this related sense, the idea of "changing" the status of the Scheduled Castes involves creative proccess intended to bring about change in their traditional status.

Although, it is believed that from the time of Buddha through Middle Ages upto nineteenth century the caste system was attacked so that social inequalities could be alleviated. But no organized attempt seems to have been made until abolition of disabilities of religion, place of birth, descent, colour, etc., as regards employment in Government; legal enactment of Indian Penal Code as far as equality of treatment in regard to the cases in the courts is concerned; declaring open the educational institutions for the Depressed Classes and issuance of instructions for withdrawal of grants paid to the aided educational institutions in case they denied admission to the Scheduled Castes students, and devising a few other measures relevant to the problems of the Scheduled Castes were effected by the British Government in the nineteenth century and the first quarter of twentieth century. Thereafter, as a result of social reform movements organized by the social reformers and Indian Nationalists during latter part of the nineteenth and early part of the twentieth century, the British Government, on the recommendations of the Simon Commission Report of 1930, incorporated them in the Government of India Act of 1935 for their development and upliftment.

However, it is only after Independence that systematic and organized efforts have been made. They have been enlisted for safeguarding against their traditional sufferings and for promoting their life situations as provided in the Constitution of India.

The design of action has been worked out in the light of various provisions made in the Constitution and the 'Directive Principles" in Article 46 of the Constitution that : "The State shall promote with special care the educational and economic interests of the weaker sections of the people and, in particular, of the Scheduled Castes and the Scheduled Tribes and shall protect them from social injustice and all forms of exploitation."

The actions designed, in compliance with the assurances given to the Scheduled Castes, constitute a series of "Protective" and "Promotive" measures considered effective in eliminating the evils of the traditional Indian society and promoting the life of the Scheduled Castes. The measures consist of the following :

(*i*) *Protective Measures* : include Constitutional and Legislative Safeguards against "untouchability" and imposition of disabilities on account of untouchability, which have been a major factor for social inequalities between the Scheduled Castes and the other groups of castes and for degradation of the Scheduled Castes. In the "Protective" measures are also included actions against exploitation and deprivation of rights and privileges. For example, Constitutionally, by Article 17, untouchability has been abolished and enforcement of any disability arising out of untouchability has been made punishable; by Article 15 (2) discrimination on grounds of caste has been prohibited; by Article 29 (2) denial of admission into educational institutions on grounds of caste has been forbidden; and by Article 23 (1) they have been protected against "Begar" and other similar forms of forced labour. As a Legislative measure against practice of untouchability and discrimination against the Scheduled Castes "Untouchability (Offences) Act 1955," now amended as "Protection of Civil Rights Act 1976" has been enforced. By this Act enforcing religious, social, educational, occupational and by other kind of disabilities, enforcing to do any invidious or similar work and denial of any rights or privileges to which they would be entitled have been made punishable offence. Besides it, "Bonded Labour System (Abolition) Act 1976" has been enforced against exploitation.

(*ii*) *Promotive Measures* : include reservation of posts in services along with certain concessions relating to examination fees, age limit, etc., financial assistance in terms of grants and loans and educational facilities in terms of reservation of seats in educational institutions, freeship, book aid, etc. for the development and upliftment of these castes. As provided by Article 16 (4) in the Constitution of India, provisions for reservation of posts in services have been made. The objective of this provision is to concretize the ideal of occupational mobility for the Scheduled Castes. Article 275 of the Constitution provides guiding principles with a view to extend assistance and facilities directed towards economic development and betterment in education, housing, health etc.

Besides these measures directly concerned with the development and upliftment of the Scheduled Castes. seats in the House of People and in the Legislative Assemblies have been reserved for them as provided in Articles 330 and 332. Seats have also been reserved to ensure representation of the Scheduled Castes in the Village Panchayats.

Moreover, to monitor all the matters relating to the advancement and upliftment of the Scheduled Castes provision for appointment of a Special Officer as provided in Article 338 and also appointment of a Commission as provided in Article 340 of the Constitution has been made.

Changing Trends

It is true that acceptance of universal franchise, adoption of Parliamentary System of Government, expansion of education, planned system for economic growth and other measures have introduced new patterns of interaction between different castes and the protective and promotive measures for the Scheduled Castes have made important social changes in the age-old patterns of life and work (Singhi, 1979 : 81). As a result of these several directed and non-directed social changes certain changes certainly taken have place in the status of the Scheduled Castes (Singhi, 1979 : 82). But, as mentioned in the Report of the Working Group on the Development of Scheduled Castes 1980-85, it is far from expectations. The Report states that "Notwithstanding Constitutional provisions and accepted policy priorities, the development effort for the Scheduled Castes has so far been too meagre to make a significant impact on the socio-economic life and almost all of them continue to be below the poverty line and suffer from the stigma and disabilities arising from the evil custom of untouchability" (1980 : 2). In a study of the Scheduled Castes of Kumaon assessing the impact of the

"Protective" and "Promotive" measures taken together, progressive trends in economic and educational status have been noted. But as regards traditional status imprecated with the stigma of untouchability and disabilities, these measures have had no appreciable impact, for, as the study revealed, discrimination against them in different socio-ritual matters is a widespread phenomenon. Even the economic advancement and spread of education are of little help in eliminating the stigma of inferiority of caste which they inherit (Maurya, 1986).

Moreover, studies and reports concerning the Scheduled Castes and also observations of practical social life indicate that most of them pursue the same traditional occupation which was a major factor leading to their degraded status in the traditional Indian Society. On the other hand, the majority of them live below the poverty line. Even the educational advancement of the Scheduled Castes has brought no important change in their traditional status. Despite change in economic status as a result of increasing occupational mobility and spread of education on account of promotive measures and also the modernizing forces, social inequalities between higher castes and the Scheduled Castes continue and the Scheduled Castes have to suffer degradation on account of the stigma of untouchability and the disabilities attached to their caste traditionally.

The inequalities based on common factors are unavoidable. But the hereditary inequalities and the tendency for perpetuating it can be checked. It may, therefore, be emphasized that changing the status of the Scheduled Castes involves checking of hereditary degradation and the tendency for prepetuating it, and also bringing them out of the vicious circle of occupations.

References

1. Davis, Kingsley, *Human Society*, The MacMillan Company, New York, 1967.
2. Desai, A.R., *Rural Sociology in India*, The Indian Society of Agricultural Economics, Bombay, 1969.
3. D'souza, Victor, *Inequality and its Perpetuation*, Manohar Publications, New Delhi, 1981.
4. Gerth, H.H. and Mills, C.W. (Trans. & eds.), *Max Weber : Essays in Sociology*, Routledge and Kegan Paul Ltd., London, E. C. 4, 1967.
5. Ghurye, G.S., *Caste and Race in India*, Popular Prakashan, Bombay, 1969.
6. Hutton, J.H., *Caste in India*, Oxford University Press, London, 1951.
7. Macdonell, A.A. and Keith, A.B , *Vedic Index of Names and Subjects*, Vol. II, Motilal Banarsidas, Delhi : Varanasi, Patna, 1958.
8. *Manusmiriti*, Randhir Book Sales (Publication), Haridwar.
9. Marriott, McKim, "*Caste Ranking and Community Structure in Five Regions of India and Pakistan*, Published in the Bulletin of the Deccan College Research Institute (B.D.C.R,I.), Poona, Vol. XIX, No. 1 & 2, 1968.
10. Maurya, R.L., *A Study of the Impact of the Planned Processes on the Life of the Scheduled Castes of Kumaon* (Unpublished), November, 1986.
11. Mayer, A.C., *Caste and Kinship in Central India*, University of California Press, Angeles, 1965.
12. Mehta, Haroobhai and Patel, Hasmukh (eds.), *Dynamics of Reservation Policy*, Patriot Publishers, New Delhi, 1985.
13. Ogburn, William F. and Nimkoff, Meyer F., *A Handbook of Sociology*, Routledge and Kegan Paul Ltd., London, 1964.
14. Parkin, Frank, *Class Inequality and Political Order : Social Stratification in Capitalist and Communist Societies*, MacGibbon and Kee, London, 1971.
15. *Govt. of India : Report of the Depressed Classes and Aboriginal Tribes Committee*, 1930.
16. *Report of the Commissioner for Scheduled Castes and Scheduled Tribes*, 1981-82.

17. *Report of the Working Group on the Development of Scheduled Castes*, 1980-85, September 1980.

18. Rose, Arnold M. and Rose, Caroline B., *Sociology : The Study of Human Relations*, Alfred A Knoff Inc., New York, 1969.

19. Ross, H. Laurence, *Perspectives on the Social Order : Readings in Sociology*, University College of Arts and Science, New York University, New York, 1963.

20. Sharma, R.S., *Sudras in Ancient India*, Motilal Banarasidas, Delhi, Varanasi, Patna, 1958.

21. Singhi, Narendra K., *Education and Social Change*, Rawat Publications, Jaipur, 1979.

SEVEN

Nutrition Problem and Diseases Caused by Malnutrition Among Scheduled Castes

(*A Case Study of Tikamgarh Tahsil of Madhya Pradesh*)

Dr. R.P. Tiwari, Dr. R.S. Tripathi
and Dr. P.D. Tiwari

Introduction

In India, the Scheduled Castes are one of the most backward group of regional development. So the Socio-economic status of Scheduled Caste population is the index of over all development of that area. Inspite of various development plans, implemented by the Government, these groups are still under-developed due to high birth rate, ill health, meagre resources for their livelihood and conservative behaviour towards different innovations. The problem becomes alarming further more when supply of various edibles is converted into various food nutrients required for the normal growth of Scheduled Caste groups. as it is not only the quantity of food nutrients, which matter quite a lot. Imbalance supply of these elements results in various nutritional problems and diseases caused by malnutrition among Scheduled Castes.

Malnutrition means strictly speaking bad nutrition which includes both excess and deficiency. In the present paper, an attempt has been made to study this problem at micro-level in Tikamgarh Tahsil of Madya Pradesh.

The Study Area

The study area, and of the five Tahsils of Tikamgarh District of Madhya Pradesh is situated in the south western part of Bundelkhand granitic region. The area is bounded on north by Jatara Tahsil and on east by Baldeogarh Tahsil of Tikamgarh district, on south east by Bijawar Tahsil of Chhatarpur District and on south west by Mahroni Tahsil of Lalitpur district of Uttar Pradesh, lying between parallels of 24° 26′ and 24° 55′ North and meridians of 80° 47′ and 81° 19′ East. The Tahsil covers an area of 1,725.10 Sq. Km. which is 16% of the district as a whole. According to its share of population (1,48,065 persons) is 20.09% of the total district population out of which 18.84% being Scheduled Caste population, the study area consists of 177 villages of 57 Patwari Halkas and three Revenue Inspector Circles. It is predominantly are agricultural region with three well marked agricultural seasons, Kharif, Rabi and Jayad.

Methodology

The part of the study is based on secondary data which has been used by field survey of the five centres (Tikamgarh city, Kari, Badagaon, Aston and Mabai villages) of the region, which has been conducted at house hold level of Scheduled Castes families through the methods of questionaires and interviews regarding diets and dietary patterns (habits). For the assessment of the nutritional (Food Stuffs) standard, the Scheduled Caste people of the above selected villages, various edibles available to them have been converted into different elements of diet with the help of a conversation table of I.C.M.R. New Delhi. Finally the available data and informations were processed and to correlate the occurance of nutritional deficiency diseases with the supply of various elements of diet for the Scheduled Castes families. This paper is modest attempt to know the availability of nutrition problems of the study area's Scheduled Caste people and their relationship between health and diseases caused by malnutrition. The suggestions for the improvement of nutritional pattern of this group has also been given in the end of the study.

Dietary Pattern

Dietary pattern of Scheduled Castes in different parts of the region have improved around local food production. Each person of this group adjusting habits and taste to domestically food stuffs. Physical factors like climate, ecology and population have exerted an important influence upon human food habits. In recent time, economic factors for Scheduled Caste group have played an important part in bringing about radical change in the character of diet.

In the area under study, agriculture is centered on production of grains, cereals constitute the bulk of the diet. Almost half of the food energy of the region in obtained from cereals, the most important in human diet because it contains protein of the highest quality, minerals such as iron, phosphorus, calcium and others alongwith some of vitamins and fats. In a small part of the region, cattles are valued for food and milk for Scheduled Caste peoples but mostly their primary purpose in ploughing fields and pulling carts. Fish is a very important food material in the diet of the regional Scheduled Caste people. The situation of the region is away for the sea and is unfavourable for fishing except in land waterways. Lakes and tanks at present are some how lying indesolation and destitute. For want of maintenance and upkeep, the capacity of lakes and tanks in the aea is rainshed. As fish is cheaper than meat, its consumption within the region is usually larger among Scheduled Castes population than the other castes.

It is observed that the Scheduled Caste people of the region begin their day with a meagre breakfast consisting of left over from the previous night's meal, locally known as 'Kaleu' at about 7'Clock in the morning. Tea is not or even just introduced in the rural areas of this group due to lack of economic development, but some families regularly take tea or mattha (Butter milk) in the breakfast. In Tikamgarh city tea is a very common item for the breakfast but most of them the use of these items is uncommon though they sometimes, take them. The lunch comparises of chapati prepared from flour of jowar or wheat or mixed flour of gram and wheat with pulses or fried potatoes. Green vegetables are rarely taken by Scheduled Caste group in the region. Some families of this group purchase the vegetables from the nearest market. The night meal called 'Biaru' consist of same food as the lunch and, in addition, includes porridge (dalia or maheree).

It has also been observed that milk and meat are not very important item in the reguler diet of Scheduled Castes people. As most of the families of this group can not afford meat for their diet is not surprising. Dhanuk, Shephered, Oilpressure and other low caste people do oceasionally take meat but they neither can afford it regularly not it is easily available. The some Scheduled Caste families, who are quite well off and who have own cattle, regularly consume milk and milk products, but most of the families of this group can not afford to have milk regularly because they have to sell the milk to supplement their income. Similarly some of the families take eggs oceasionally.

One of the chief characteristic features of regional village dietary is that various types of cereals, pulses and vegetables provide a variation in food of the Scheduled Caste in different seasons. Majority of these families use course cereals such as barley, gram millet etc. from September to March millet and rice form chief incomponents of food because they are profusely available after the Kharif harvest, from April, gram and wheat are used in the preparation of bread. Rice is often used in the Scheduled Caste families because rice is not a complete diet in the region, but is taken as a supplementary food article, especially in the evening meals.

Food Stuffs

Although the present level of food consumption is not fully known, estimate indicates that the region is more or less self sufficient in food production and intake of calories is not the yardstick of measuring good health. Consumption of food over 2,000 calories does not necessarily meant that all is well. Even with a high caloric intake a person may suffer from several specific nutritional diseases, caused due to lack of nutritive element in diet, i.e. protiens, carbohydrate, fat, vitamins and minerals. Calories, the chief source of providing energy to the body is simply a quantitative rather than a qualitative measurement of food. Most diseases occur due to deficiency of protein of animals origin and vitamins.

Protein

Protein supplies the building material for body and makes good the wear and tear of tissues which is a constant feature of the process of life. It is actually indispensable for the normal constituents of every cell in the process of life. It is a typical nitro-carbolic compound plays a vital role to development in the human body.

Carbohydrate

Carbohydrate supplies direct energy to the body. The requirement of this edible is very important for the hard working persons. The sugar, milk, fruits and glucose are rich by carbohydrate.

Fats

The deficiency of fat does not directly result in any disease but it aggravates various deficiency diseases. For every nutrient has its own importance for human body. Fat is rich in milk and animals. Excess of fat in the human body is more harmful than the lack of this edible.

Vitamins

Vitamins are the essential constituents of food plant act in the human body as a digestive material. Vitamins are essential carbon compound of the nature, known as accessory dietary factors of the human body.

Minerals

A comparative measure of judge the nutritional standard of the people calories are no doubt a base, but it can not be the only basis to give a clear picture of the nutrition and health, because nutritionally an adequate diet should also contain proportionate amount of minerals like calcium, iodine, iron, phosporus and others.

A good health is a result of a balanced diet that consist of right proportions of protiens, fats, carbohydrates, vitamins and mineral in each group of population, because proteins are needed to built and repair the body tissues, fats and carbohydrates to provide energy and vitamins and minerals to regulate the body processes. Through the study of five selected centres of the region it has been found that protein and other food stuff requirements of various Scheduled Caste population are not the same and are influenced by physiological conditions like growth, pregnancy and lactation. Table 1 shows the comparative position of consumption of food stuffs in Tikamgarh Tahsil.

According to table 1 the caloric intake of Scheduled Caste and low income groups point out all caster under study recieved less calories (average-695) as recommended by Food and Nutritional Board of India. The average caloric intake of given castes are 1705 unit only, in which the highest (1934) in Kachhi, followed by Dheemer (1904) and lowest in shephered (1039).

TABLE 1

Comparative Position of Consumption of Food Stuff (Per Head Per Day) in Different Low/ Scheduled Castes Population in Tikamgarh Tahsil

S.N.	*Castes*	*Calories*	*Proteins in Grm.*	*Percentage of Proteins*		*Fats (Grm.)*	*Carbohydrates (Grm.)*
				Vegetable	*Animals*		
1	2	3	4	5	6	7	8
1.	Kachhi	1934	47.34	93.30	6.70	36.12	390.44
2.	Dheemar	1904	57.91	84.40	14.60	34.39	367.19
3.	Dhanuk	1831	43.66	92.34	7.86	39.12	371.57
4.	Shephered	1039	39.99	92.04	7.96	40.10	321.29
5.	Leather worker	1730	43.35	89.16	10.84	37.44	344.47
6.	Sweeper	1634	40.99	91.89	8.21	32.38	313.85
7.	Oil pressure	1667	39.36	96.30	3.70	48.49	399.70
8.	Bhurji	1793	31.31	100.00	—	42.72	378.35
9.	Potters	1788	32.77	90.50	9.50	35.58	361.28
10.	Washerman	1877	41.38	91.81	8.19	37.27	344.52
	Average	1705	41.81	92.17	7.83	38.36	359.26

Vitamins			Minerals			Caloric
A I.U.	*B I.U.*	*C Grm.*	*Calcium*	*Iron*	*Phosphores*	*Deficiency*
9	10	11	12	13	14	15
3344	1.77	178	0.785	32.10	0.840	— 466
3640	1.68	182	0.732	31.31	0.822	— 496
3489	1.64	181	0.688	30.82	0.891	— 569
3013	1.59	173	0.622	29.14	0.744	—1361
3140	1.68	176	0.643	29.48	0.748	— 670
3089	1.73	181	0.711	31.22	0.799	— 766
3744	1.84	192	0.800	32.90	0.900	— 733
3510	1.81	190	0.822	32.19	0.901	— 707
3404	1.64	191	0.791	31.89	0.888	— 662
3101	1.66	184	0.699	30.72	0.823	— 523
3347	1.70	183	0.729	31.18	0.835	— 695

Caste wise comparative food suff analysis shows that the Dheemer caste is better in protein intake than the other low castes of the region due to taking of animal protein, while Dhanuk, Washerman Shephered, Leather workers, potters, sweapers and other low castes receiving very low quantity of protien because of undeveloped economic conditions and backwardness. According to protein analysis the data clearly reveals that the percentage of animal protein is quite unsatisfactory (Average 7.83% only), Dheemar (14.60%), leather worker (10.84%) and potters (9.50%) are taking the animal protein occasionally and according to their income. The average fats intake in Scheduled Caste population is only 38.36 Grm. only and carbohydrate 359.26 Grm., which is quite low and caused nutrition problem. The same conditions is still standing of taking of vitamins and minerals proportion in the diet of this group. The economic condition play a vital role in the development of nutrition pattern.

During the period of pregnancy among women not only the intake of proteins should be emphasised in adequate quantity but at the same time minerals and vitamins in sufficient quantity are also required. The diet of Scheduled Caste population in this region is predominatly imbalanced. Since nothing is done in thie regard in the region, hence poor growth of Scheduled Caste children with much lower resistance. No special treatment of the young children is in general in practice in the study area. Vegetables and fruits are not out standing sources of carotene. Vitamin 'B' and 'C' and minerals Calcium and Iron. Poor body structure of the most of the children of this group is often attributed to low calcium intakes. There is a wide prevalance of iron deficiency among women of child bearing age. Carbohydrates and fats supply energy for every movement, from heart beat to all the movements of the organism in routine work and recreation. The foods rich in these nutrients are fats (ghee, oil, butter, cream etc.) The sugars (sugar, taggery, honey, jams etc.) flour potatoes oatoneal and other cereals. These nutrients are rarely available in low income group families of Scheduled

Castes. So very low quantity has been taken by this group in the study area.

Malnutrition

The problem of protein-Caloric malnutrition the Scheduled Castes in wide spread almost throughout the region though different degrees in different parts. Available evidences indicate that severe degrees of protein Caloric have been marked all over the region because rice cultivation is a common factor. The only fully satisfactory sources of these are meat dairy products and eggs. But these items are lacking in the diet of or Scheduled Castes population resulting in serious protein deficiency.

The problem of malnutrition in Scheduled Caste in the region is of special concern among pregnant and nursing women and infants. In the region Scheduled Castes children are insufficiently fed at home, school feeding programmes may help to make up vitamins and other nutritional deficiencies. The socio-cultural heritage of this group is adversely attached with traditional backwardness. Among the cultural factors superstitious old moral values, customs and religious taboos are also important in determining the direct dietary pattern among the poor and illiterate persons in Scheduled Castes causing protein deficiency and malnutrition diseases. But it is mainly malnutrition is responsible for high incidence of foetal deaths. Malnutrition in this regard is more prevalent in children and women rather than men of Scheduled Caste population. Prolonged severe malnutrition may even impair the bodies capacity to benefit from an improved diet. Malnutrition reflects the inadequacy in the nutritional quality of the diet. Table 2 shows deficiency diseases caused by malnutrition the various food stuffs.

Table 2 reveals that deficiency in food stuffs leads to various diseases which in turn, account for lower resistance to infections of which the rural Scheduled Caste people become

TABLE 2

Deficiency Disease Casused by Malnutrition

S. N.	Food Stuffs		Deficiency Diseases
1.	Protein		Hypoprotonaemia and Kwashiorkor.
2.	Carbohydrates		Weakness and loss of weight.
3.	Fats		It does not directly result in any disease but it aggravates various deficiency diseases.
4.	Vitamins	'A'	'X' Hyperkeratinization of skin at large and the keratinizing metaplasm in the beginning of the respiratory organs, gastro-intestinal and genitourinary tract, Night blindness, Xeroderma and Stomatitis, Keratomelacia etc.
		'B'	Chronic dierrhoea and Pellegra.
		'C'	Pyorrhea and dental carries, Swelling in various parts in the body.
		'D'	Skin affection, fragility of bones and scurby.
5.	Thiamine		Constipation and Beriberi.
6.	Riboflaevin		Fissures at the angle of mouth and local inflammation, desquamation and escrustation angular stomatitis and glossites.
7.	Minerals-	Calcium—	Dental decay, reckets and ostomalacia.
		Iron—	Anaemia.
		Phosphorus—	Stunting
		Iodine—	Goitre, Cretimism and dwarfishness.

easy victims. In this connection the most important point to be realised is that most of the diseases result due to the lack of multiple nutrients rather than the deficiency of any one of them. However, the dietary surveys carried out by the authority has selected five centres of the region shown that the diet of the considerable portion of Scheduled Caste population is inadequate both quantitatively and qualitatively. The diet of the regional Scheduled Caste people is not only qualitative by embalanced, as shown above but also quantitatively insufficient. All the Scheduled Castes population of the area under study depends on small quantities of food which does not provide the basic reguirement of calories. It has been found that the regional Scheduled Caste population constantly lives on the varge of hunger which directly crushes the physical efficiency of labours. It is a vicious circle the people are under feed or ill-fed, they have no reserves of physical strength so they become easy prey to diseases and turn out as subject to cronic lessitude, lacking energy and cannot labour hard. This leads to agricultural insufficiency and back to undernourishment of Scheduled Castes. As stated by C.E.A. Winsiowman, women are sick because they are poor; they become poor because they are sick they were sick and sicker because they were poorer.

Causes Of Malnutrition

There are many great causes of malnutrition in the region. Here are some of the most important ones.

1. Careless use of natural and economic resources.
2. Continuous growth of population.
3. Primitive type of agricultural patterns.
4. Poor cattle breading.
5. Undeveloped fishing industry.
6. Lack of industrial development.
7. Lack of transport facilities.
8. Dirty nature and poor standard of living of Schedule Caste families.
9. Poor nourishment of children-especially in female child.

10. Lack of educational facilities.
11. Lack of Government planning.
12. Problem of traditional pattern etc.

Suggeestions for the Improvements of Nutritional Pattern

Malnutrition is widely prevalent in the region particularly the Scheduled Caste families of the rural areas. A study of malnutritional problems in Scheduled Caste population based on geographical and cultural environment, will be more effective in eliminating nutritional problems. There is however much scope for further progress in the solution of malnutrition as well as improvement of dietary health of the region.

1. Limiting of family size.
2. Increase in food production and to investigate new source of food production such as food yeast utilization.
3. To extract food directly from green plants requires further investigation.
4. Education about balanced diet.
5. Ascertaining of fundamental roles of particularly dietary constituents.
6. Improvements of financial conditions.
7. Development of new methods of cooking and preparing food.
8. Changing the habits of Scheduled Caste, all castes (People) Vegetarian to non-vegetarian.
9. More manuring of soil.
10. Development of irrigational facilities.
11. Scientific improvements of agriculture.
12. Plant protection and anti-plant disease schemes.
13. Development of Pisciculture.

14. Opening of Balwadi, Anganwadi and other social welfare programmes.
15. Change in age structure.
16. School meal programme would be re-implemented.
17. Need of integrated services for nutrition in Scheduled Castes population.

References

1. Ackroyd W.R. (1962) Gopalan C. and Subramanyan S.C. — *The Nutritive Value of Indian Food and the Planning of Satisfactory Diet*, I.C.M,R., New Delhi, pp. 49-55.
2. Bose P.K. (1977) — *Population Food-Nutrition Equation in India*, Everymens Science Vol. XII No. 1 pp. 17-34.
3. F.A.O., (1964) — *Food Consumption Tables for International Use.*
4. Mohammad Noor (ed.), (1980) — *Nutritions and Nutritional Deficiency Diseases in Ghaghra-Rapti Doab*, Perspective Agricultural Geog. Human Dimensions in Agriculture Vol. V, New Delhi, PP. 179-194.
5. Sen A.K. (1973) — *Nutrition and Population Education*, P.E. Unit Department of Social Sciences and Humanities, National Institute of Education N.C.E.R.T., New Delhi-16.
6. Sen S.N. (1976) — *Nutrition and Rural Development Some Economic Aspects Everymens Science*, Volume XI, No. 1, pp. 33-43.
7. Sharma S.C. (1972) — *Land Use and Nutrition in Village Manikpur in the Central Upland of the Lower Yamuna Chambal Doab*, Geographical

Review of India, Vol. 34, No. 4, pp. 368-385.

8. Shukla P.N. (1986) — *Nutritional Deficiency and Diseases*, A Case Study of Ravives Village Jaitpur Distt. Etawah (U.P.) Transactions I.C.G. Vol. 16, Jan. 86, pp. 15-22.

9. Singh B.B. (1968) — *The Availability of Calories Available for Food in the Villages*, Block Baraut of Distt. Meerut. The Geographical Observes Vol. 4, M.C.G.S., pp. 66-77.

EIGHT

On the Problems of Scheduled Castes Observations of Harijan Elites

Dr. R.C. Dwivedi

At present, Scheduled Castes are facing various problems in a position of dilemma because the diffusion of modernization has eroded the lawfulness of the traditional social order in which Scheduled Castes were living a life bereft of dignity and marked by great poverty, exploitation and oppreision. This erosion has brought two things to the home of untouchables : One, the inequitous and unjust situation of the traditional social order and two, a new social order based on equality and justice can be brought about; or, at least, the Scheduled Castes can transcend their traditional handicaps and enjoy a better socio-economic status.

In a democratic political country like India, the lever of the transformation of the social system or the transcendence of the handicaps by the untouchables is a political action. But, through political action, the Scheduled Castes are mere taking advantage of reservation in education, services, etc. While other obstacles like economic security, equality and dignity are still in vague, hammering the lives of Harijans. It also excites reaction from the higher castes blocking the advance of the Scheduled Castes on the slippery path of socio-economic status upgradation.

Confronted by this hostile environment, the Scheduled Castes are compelled to oscillate between two poles of rebellion and silence. Appointing to the Harijan Elites as the vanguard of the Scheduled Castes, their perception have been very useful for gaining a deeper insight into the various apects of the existence of the Harijans. The elites are also expected not only to give the advice but also to actively engage in finding a solution of various problems as a "friend, philospher and guide." Activities of the elites are, therefore, no doubt very important. With this background in mind this study attempts to deal with Harijan Elites.

Untouchability is, no doubt, a social poison. However, it becomes highly injurious when those whose touch is supposed to be polluting, are themselves treated as social dross and ship wrecked person. As Owen M-Lynch puts it :

> For centuries India's untochables have been one of the world's most down trodden and oppressed minorities. They lived in hamlets segregated from other villagers; were not allowed to use the wells of upper castes or to share food with them; were denied access to temples, priests and Sanskrit knowledge of Hinduism; were forbidden to dress, use jwelery, and display symbols reserved for upper castes alone; and were basically landless and poorest of the poor. They were non-persons stereotyped as ignorant, hereditarily incompetent, and morally inferior and impure.[1]

While untouchable Castes toil to supply many socially and economically useful benefits to prerogative groups, collect foul matter, refuse, fragments and slurs on behalf of society, have themselves been made the chief emblem of social refuse for more than two thousand years. True picture of the status of social refuse has been depicted by Dr. B.R. Ambedkar in the following lines :

"Untouchables are as a case of exploitation without obligation. For him, the Hindus have a vested interest in keeping the institution of untouchability intact. Hindus have been exploiting the untouchables and, what is more sordid, they have been experiencing pride and dignity befitting a master class at the cost of the untouchables. The untouchables have been used as forced labourers, scavengers and sweepers because they could be compelled due to their state of complete destitution and helplessness to work on a mere pittance and sometimes on nothing at all."[2]

Indian society has been distinguished by what is called "cumulative inequality." The partition of the society into 'varnas' and 'Jatis,' whatever may have been its origin alludes to a special model of the allotment of strength and prosperity. Various social reformers have accepted the origin of varnavyavastha according to Aryan Culture. But Dr. Ambedkar on the other hand, rejects the theory of Aryan colonisation and attributes the relegation of the Shudras. According to him, "There were originally only three Varnas (Brahmines, Kshatriyas and Vaishayas) and that the Shudras were only a part of the second varna.... The degradation of the Shudra was the result of a violent conflict between the Shudras and Brahmins."[3]

Criticizing the Brahmins, Dr. Ambedkar observes, "The Brahmin systematically preyed on society and profiteered in religion. The Puranas and Shastras he manufactured are treasure trove of sharp practices which the Brahmins employed to fool, beguil and suindle the common mass of poor, illitrate and superstitious Hindus."[4] Further, he observes caustically, "Brahmin is the poison which has spoiled Hinduism. You will succeed in saving Hinduism if you will kill Brahminism."[5] In mounting a Vigorous attack ou Brahminism, his main concern had all along been the injustices done to the untouchables. He emphatically told them, "Never regard yourselves as untouchables. Live a clean life and educate, agitate and organise" yourself to get what is due to you.

Similarly, Jagjivan Ram agrees with Dr. Ambedkar and believes, "When the Aryans entered India, they had outgrown the stage of tribal endogamy. Among them there were only three divisions conforming to the three primitive functional divisions of priests, warriors and artisans. Varna in this trivarnic society indicated a particular social function and a distinct level of culture and a way of life. The clash between the Aryan invaders and aboriginal inhabitants of India accentuated not only the cultural but even the occupational and functional divisions. A fourth caste, the shudras, came into being. Society became chaturvarnic. The sages sang of its eternal nature. Men gradually came to believe that the order was divinely ordained."[7]

Further, this pattern of distribution, according to aforesaid varnavyavastha, sharpens to the reality that the different phases of socio-economic status ranking, instead of being widely partaken by the people, tend to concentrate at the higher rungs of status hierarchy. Only, the location of a upper caste person has been instrumental in his acquiring a larger capital for maintaining his llfe-condition and his progeny's life-chances. Due to wealth and social reputation of higher caste person, he enjoyed political power too. His convergence of prosperity and power towards upper castes meant that low status groups were deprived of enjoying in any remarkable manner these benefits. As a consequence of this, they were debarred from participating in any meaningful way in social operations.

The socio-economic status hierarchy would not have been so oppressive if the boundaries dividing different jatis had not been harshly drawn and scrupulously respected. As Dr. Ambedkar puts it :

In slavery, the master at any rate had the responsibility to feed, clothe and house the slave and keep him in a good condition lest the market value of the slave should decrease, lest in the system of untouchability the Hindu takes on responsibility for the maintenance of the untouchables. As an economic system it permits exploitation without obligation,[8] Ambedkar further observes.

Untouchability is not only a system of unimigated economic exploitation, but it is also a system of uncontrolled economic exploitation. That is because there is no independent public opinion to condemn it and there is no impartial machinery of administration to restrain it. There is no appeal to public opinion for whatever public opinion there is, it is the opinion of the Hindus who belong to the exploiting class and as such favour exploitation. There is no check from the police or the judiciary for the simple reason that they are all drawn from the Hindus, and take the side of exploiters.[9]

As a part of the traditional social order, the untouchables were excluded from becoming partners in the process of history-making. Jagjivan Ram emphasizes :

"All achievements of India and all her successes were confined only to the upper castes. The masses constituting the lower classes were made to work for the advancement of society but were excluded from being partners in the process of history-making. They were deliberately kept outside history. Thus, they were outside creative national endeavours.[10]

The Hindu society did not stop here. It developed highly finished principles and rules covering all phases of life. It formulated that the inequality according to castes were supposed to be ordained by God. In this way, the inequality in Hindu society was supported by religion and the theories of transmigration and of Karma. The seriousness of this ideology was so perfect that even Harijans who were most-adversely affected by this social order did not question its accuracy Remarking on the mentality of the untouchables, Jagjivan Ram says: "The complete mental conditioning had eliminated all sense of revolt from the minds of the majority, which had to tail not only for its own upkeep but for the upkeep of the exploiting upper castes. Even the untouchables believed that if they carried on their duties in this life, which were ordained by providence, uncomplainingly, willingly and obediently they would probably be born in a higher group in their next birth."[11]

Although, gradual thinking that all men are born free and equal had originated among human personality. But this perception of thinking did not provoke so much. However various religious protest movements highlighted the extensive gap between the distinctive belief of Hinduism and its unbearable traditions. But these movements failed to make any effective dent in the fortress of Hindu orthodoxy and obstinacy.

However, the advent of British Rule trembled the roots of insufferable practices of Hinduism. It was done by the creation of new opportunities of physical and occupational mobility. But the real Scheduled Castes village area remained conservative and faithful to the Hindu religion. Accepting it, Jagjivan Ram says :

> Indian Village economy and its more or less self-sufficient character received to killing blow when machine-made or mill-made commodities started competing with hand made products. When industrial regions started expanding, pauperized agricultural worker or peasantry and even the artisans were drawn to these industrial centres. The methods of imperalistic exploitation dictated that the village should produce nothing except the primary commodities which could be used as raw materials by the manufacturing industries. The advent of industrial life and the effects of industrialization helped to reduce the rigours of the caste

system in the urban areas, but the villages remained conservative and faithful to the Hiudu system of thought.[12]

While Dr. Ambedkar made it clear that no Government even the British Government did not do anything for the miseries of the Scheduled Castes. Speaking at the First Round Table Conference in 1928, he said :

> Indeed, so far as we are concerned, the British Government has accepted the social arrangements as it found them, and has preserved them faithfully in the manner of a Chinese Tailor who, when given and old ccat as a pattern, produced with pride an exact replica, rents, patches and all. Our wrongs have remained as open sores as they have not been righted, although 150 years of British rule have rolled away. It was not merely a case of indifference, rather it was a case of sheer importance to undertake the task.[13]

In fact, the collision of the British Raj on Indian society was much intensive, rather than the creation of new opportunities to depressed class. No doubt, they constituted alternative channels of organizing life, shaping life conditions and influencing life-chance. Furthermore, they were instrumental in breaking the rigidity of hereditary occupational patterns and loosening the stranglehold of the Hindu social order on the deprived and the destitute. In this way they provided a new ray of hope, confidence and equal democratic power to the untouchables.

However, in British Raj period a violent hurricane for 'Independent India' came. There was also a reformist movement led by Jotirao Phule in mid-nineteenth century and later by Gandni and Dr. Ambedkar during the peak of freedom movement which did culminate safeguards to the untouchables. In all this Gandhi's role comes for a bitter criticism. To most of them, Dr. Ambedkar was a man with forsight. While fighting for the cause of the down-trodden people, he was fully aware of the problems facing the Scheduled Castes today. That is why he advocated separate electorate which was, in fact, granted by the Mac-Donald Communal Awards. But Gandhi shot this Award down by declaring his intention to undertake a fast up to death against it. Ultimately, Gandhi's views prevailed and a historic 'Poona Pact, 1932' was signed.[14] Had this not happened, the fate of the Scheduled Caste leadership would have been much different, instead of the bonded nature of the present leadership.

India became independent after a long struggle but the fate of the untouchables was still in dark. Although, Independent India brings to the Scheduled Castes, a message of a new dawn tinged brilliantly with the promise of a better and dignified life free of wants. True measures under the rubric of "protective discrimination" have been undertaken to help them. Dr. Ambedkar was very much aware of the handicaps of Scheduled Castes. That is why he, while opting for Parliamentary democracy prefers to prescribe state socialism by the law of the Constitution, so that it will be beyond the approch of a Parliamentary majority to suspend, amend or abrogate it. It is only by this that, Dr. Ambedkar believes, "One can achieve the triple object, namely, to establish socialism, retain Parliamentary democracy and avoid dictatorship."[15] Dr. Ambedkar knew that it is not enough to rely on constitutional guarantees like a non democratic society of India unless they are backed by a "constitutional morality." Jagjivan Ram was also afraid of the same happenings. As he puts :

> Today even after the approval of the Constitution, Sankaracharya can write an article saying that according to the Vedas, the Vedic temple gets polluted if person of low castes enter therein. In this way, he says, evil spirits get into the idols of the temples, and when these idols are worshipped, these evil forces become mighty.... Thus the people face destruction,[16]

Hence, Ambedkar refers to two other factors that impinge on the working of a democratic constitution :

> One is that the form of administration has a close connection with the form of the constitution. The form of the administration must be appropriate to and in the same sense as the form of the constitution. The other is that it is perfectly possible to pervert the constitution, without changing its form by merely changing the form of the administration and to make it inconsistent and opposed to the spirit of the constitution.[17]

But what does prevent the misapplication of a constitutional democracy. Ambedkar, therefore, talks of certain precedent conditions for the successful working of democracy, one of which is that :—

> There must be no glaring inequalities in the society. There must not be an oppressed class. There must not be a suppressed class. There must not be a class which has got all the privileges and a class which has got all the burdens to carry. Such a thing, such a division, such an organization of society has within itself the germs of a impossible bloody revolution and perhaps it would be impossible for democracy to cure them.[18]

In this eventuality, Ambedkar insists that the society must be based on the principles of liberty, equality and fraternity in order to ensure social endosmosis. Only in a dynamic society where changes taking place in one part are conveyed through various channels to the remaining segments can social endosmosis be effective and meaningful.[19]

What is interesting to note here is that the values which are necessary and infrastructural to the success of society are lacking in the Indian Social scenario.

Hence for the upliftment of the society and particularly untouchables, "the implementation of a pragmatic concern requires resources of various of kinds-resources like education ; appropriate skills, pragmatic, instrumental orientation, flexibility, adoptability, political strength etc. To achieve success in life's struggle—a struggle that must now be waged with modern weapons and at several levels – involves a single minded pursuit of self-interest. It brings into play the conscious processes of social calculation, tactic, judgment and management of one's economic and political resources."[20] For providing a rightful place to the untouchables in Indian Society three factors assume critical importance. First is the fundamental assumption about the individual. The Individual must be considered as autonomous rather than the bearer of certain attributes of the group he may belong to. Second is to provide the resources for certain economic needs of the individual. And, lastly, the removal of handicaps and the accrual of benefits may not be fast enough and sufficient enough to provide relief to the untouchables to the extent that they need and desire it.

It is obvious to point out that Ambedkar's role in safeguarding and promoting the interests of untouchables receives praise in all respects. He was the only Harijan elite who laid the foundation for overall socio-economic upliftment of the untouchables. Every Harijan elites admires his sharp legal mind, ability in organizing all Dalits, and his courageous leadership in launching Satyagraha. Jagjivan Ram's role is insignificant for the well being of the Scheduled Castes. Other leaders like Ram Dhan, B.P. Maurya, Ram Bilas Paswan and Kashi Ram (Bahujan Samaj Party of Uttar Pradesh) are mentioned self-centred, incompetent and are least concerned with the well-being of the Scheduled Castes. They are bonded leaders of their political parties.

They biggest problem today is that there is no such leader like Ambedkar who can guide the destiny of the Scheduled Castes and fight for them. It is, therefore, suggested that the Harijan leaders must draw lessons from Ambedkar's life and follow him. Further, they should change thier outlook and provide constructive leadership to the community. If the Scheduled Castes want improvement in their present depressing condition, they have to rise, organize and assert. Obviously, the leaders of the Schedu'ed Castes have a lot to do in this connection.

Thus the untouchables are caught in a series of dilemmas and unless they resolve these delemmas, their future will remain uncertain, ambiguous and troubled. It is against this wider back-drop that we must locate the study of Harijan elites. The Harijan elites are the most knowledgeable, articulate and advanced sector of the untouchables. The elites represent the Scheduled Caste people as a link between themselves and the external environment. They are also befitting in finding solutions to the problems.

Their experiences and thoughtful suggestions must be taken into account while framing the policies of Scheduled Caste development.

References

1. Owen M. Lynch. *Democracy in Search of Equality* : Untouchables Politics and Indian Social Change, (Delhi : Hindustan Publishing Corporation, p. 5, 1982).
2. B.R. Ambedkar, quoted in G. S. Lokhande, *Bhimrao Ranji Ambedkar* : *A Study in Social Democracy*, (New Delhi, Sterling Publishers Pvt. Ltd., p. 29, 1977).
3. Ibid, p. 77
4. B.R. Ambedkar; *Rannade, Gandhi and Jinnah.* (Bombay : Thacker and Co. Ltd., p. 20, 1943).
5. B.R. Ambedkar, *Annihilation of Caste* (Jullundher : Bheem Patrica Publications, p. 32, 1968).
6. Quoted in Lokhande, op. cit., p. 32.
7. Jagjivan Ram, *Caste Challenge in India*, (New Delhi, Vision Book Pvt. Ltd., pp. 9-10, 1980).

8. Quoted in Lokhande, op. cit. p. 30.
9. Quoted in Ibid; p. 30.
10. Jagjivan Ram, op. cit. pp. 14-15.
11. Ibid, p. 12.
12. Jagjivan Ram; op. cit., p. 12.
13. Quoted in Lokhande., op. cit., pp. 25-26.
14. For further details, see G.S. Lokhandem op. cit.
15. Ibid, p. 12.
16. Jagjivan Ram, op. cit. p. 24.
17. Quoted in Lokhande, op. cit. p. 13.
18. Ibid, p. 24.
19. Loc. cit.
20. R.S. Khare, *The Untouchable As Himself*: Ideology, Identity and Pragmatism Among the Lucknow Chamars (Cambridge ; Cambridge University Press, p 94, 1984).

NINE

Harijans : Their Conversion and Problems

Prof. A. Satyanarayana Moorty
and Dr. M.P. Narasimha Raju

Before talking anything about Harijans, it is our duty first to mention the name of Mahatma Gandhi, who popularised the term Harijans. The children of God—instead of untouchables the caste people of Malas and Madigas. However, in reality the concept of Harijan was first initiated and introduced by Saint Narashimha Mehta for the people of Scheduled Castes in India. The history of Harijans in ancient India is of miserable story of shame and sorrow, harassment and humiliation, oppression and suppression, poverty and pity.

The problem of Harijans in India is not merely a social or religious, political or economic one. It is a multifarious involving several factors. In fact, it is the baffling national problem posing a great challenge to the political leaders, administrators, sociologists, intellectuals and people of India. It is an important gigantic problem that has no parell in the history of Indian civilization. The plight of more than a hundred million

Harijans is indeed, a sad commentary on Hindu religion and Hindu culture.

Efforts were no doubt made in the past by several sociologists, social reformers, political and religious leaders, social anthropologists and social workers to redeem them to the level of the other sections of Hindu society. But these efforts could ribble at the fringe of the problems because the backwardness of these people forms a regular characteristic feature of the social fabric and any disturbance to this feature means disturbance to the entire social system.

It is left to the father of nation Mahatma Gandhi to take up the course of these people. For the first time in the history of India, he stirred up the consciousness of people against the down-trodden condition of the people. The cause of Harijans became a mass movement. The entry of Harijans into Hindu temples was a great revolution and a great achievement which the other leaders in the past could not do. It may be said that Mahatma Gandhi delivered the Harijans from the Yoke of Hindu oppression and he delivered India from the thraldom of the British. His services to the Harijans will be remembered as long as society losts.

After India got freedom many commissions and committees were appointed by both Central and State Governments to study the conditions of these people and suggested measures for their upliftment. The reports of these commissions and committees become voluminous when collected together. On the suggestions of these committees both Central and State Governments have taken many measures to ameliorate the lot of these people, provision of reservations for admissions into educational institutions at all levels and appointments in the services of the Government are incorporated in the Constitution of India. Young boys and girls who belong to Harijan community have wide spread opportunities in the spheres of education and employment.

In India, Harijans are the one of the depressed caste people. Sociological studies on them are very much fewer in number than of other social groups. But some little information about their life styles and cultures are sporadically recorded in Government official papers. Some of the authors like Thurston. Roy Burman and Balasurya Prasad have recorded certain general characteristic features on the socio-economic, political and religious features of the Scheduled Castes in India. These accounts have been drawn heavily from the occasional papers and census reports. In India full length exhaustive ethnographic reports have been published on the Chamars in 1920 by Brigg. He dealt with the cultural aspects of the Chamars of Uttar Pradesh.

After India's Independence a very few publications have been published mainly by sociologists and rarely by social anthropologists. Among these specifically mention may be noted that of the late Dr. B.R. Ambedkar (1972). He himself a politician, intellectual and also a member of these depressed classes and according to him the Sudras were Aryans belonged to the Kshatriya class. In the book 'The Coildren of Hari,' Stephen Fuchs (1949) has concentrated all the aspects of the life of Balahis in the Nimar district of Madhya Pradesh. Sachchidananda has tried to analyse their status, mobility and role transformation in his book 'Harijan Elite' (1977). I. P. Deasi's work of untouchability in Rural Gujarath is a full length discussion on untouchability based on the conception of Pollution, religious and secular sanctions in rural parts of Gujarat. Sunanda Patwardhan's study mainly deals with the analysis of change as well as continuity at behavioural, and socio-cultural levels. B.S. Moorthy has explained the problems of Harijans in his book 'Depressed and Oppressed,' and tries to solve the problems faced by them. Trivedhi H.R. (1976) has analysed the superstition, ignorance and poverty and also dealt with the exploration of the Scheduled Caste women for immoral traffic in human flesh in his book entitled, "Scheduled Caste-Women Studies in Exploitation." Dr. L.P. Vidhyarthi and

Dr. N. Misra, in their book 'Harijan Today' throw a light on socio-economic, religious, political and cultural life of the Harijans from the two cultural and linguistic zones (Magahi and Tribal) of Bihar. As a sociologist I am a late comer in the field of the subject of Scheduled Castes.' In the year 1977 the Department of Sociology in Sri Venkateswara University has introduced for the first time in Post-graduate courses a special paper on 'Harijan-Girijan Studies and also encouraged research on this subject.

Origin of Harijans as a Caste

One of the historical legacies of the Aryan conquest of India is the caste system which has its origin under certain political, economic and religious conditions. For the entire world, caste in India is a strange phenomena, an intricate social matrix which is difficult to understand. Long ago caste became a permanent social institution in India and even now it pervades the whole life of man born in India. As such, it shadows every Hindu wherever he goes.

It is hardly possible to trace the origin of the caste system with any definitness. It may have been a pre-Aryan institution, a development of pre-historic clanlife. When the Aryans came to India, they may have found caste as a very useful and convenient institution for the adjustment and maintenance of race relationships. They may have utilised the principles of caste and thereafter divided the Aryan community into four fundamental groups called 'Varnas.' The fundamental division gave raise to various varnas with which the passage of time crystalised themselves into four important groups. Finally those who were outside these four-fold classification were called Panchamas the fifth group and also known as untouchables or unapproachables or unseeables.

The untouchables call themselves as the "Depressed Caste," or "Exterior Castes," i.e., outside the caste system, 'Antyaja,'

'Asprusya,' developing communities, etc., in the different parts of the country, by a major bulk of our population. Those people who have violated the then existing caste rules are declared outlaws by caste heads. The violators are denied social intercourse with their own caste members. They are not permitted to take up the occupation of the caste. The other caste members also derived social intercourse to the violaters and not allowed them to take up the occupations of their castes. They are denied even food and drink, and asked to move out of the village. To live, the violators took to eating of dead animal's meat, and took 'unclean' occupations. Thus they have fetched the name by other members as "untouchables." Generally the Harijans live in unhealthy surroundings, eat filthy food, perform unclean duties. Hence they have been separated from the traditional Hindu society and are termed as untouchables. Because of their lower status and position, they are segregated and are made to live at the outskirts of the village completely away from the main stream of the Hindu society. Due to all these, these people are deprived of using public wells, tanks, bathing ghats, hotels, etc. and are forbidden entrance into temples and places of public worship etc. Harijans have continuous interactions with other upper caste people. They have remain segregated comparatively for a long period.

Problems of Harijans in India

The problems faced by the Harijans are classified as structural and cultural.

Structural Problems : The structural problems of Harijans are both internal and external. Internally the Harijans are cleavaged among themselves. There is a well established hierarchy in the Harijan Caste group. For example, in the state of Andhra Pradesh, the Madigas one of the major Scheduled Caste groups are lower than Malas in Social status and there is untouchability coinciding with a particular Harijan Caste position in that hierarchy. For instance the Madigas are untouchables to the Malas; while both Malas and Madigas are untouchables to the non-Harijans Castes, i.e., (i) untouchability among untouchables; & (ii) untouchability for non-untouchables. These internal differences are the first and the foremost stumbling blocks in the way of the progress of Harijans.

The external problems are multifarious. They are faced in socio-economic, political, religious and other aspects of societal life.

Cultural Problems: Among the Scheduled Castes, the cultural problems emanate from the structural position of the Harijans in the Hindu Caste hierarchy. Their material and non-material culture is different to a greater degree from that of the higher castes. Once the structural problems of the Harijans are tackled, the cultural problems will be automatically solved.

Harijans in Andhra Pradesh

Andhra Pradesh is one of the larget states in India. It has a population of 5,35,92,605 (5.35 crores) approximately covering an area of 2,77,000 square K.M. According to the census report of 1981 the total Harijan population of the state covering 6J main groups, is 60,50,000; making a percentage of 12 per cent approximately of the state total population and 14.60 per cent of the country's total population of the 58 lakhs population of Harijans in the State of Andhra Pradesh 88.4 per cent lives in rural regions. This large segment as all of us know is backward socially, economically and culturally through centuries.

The reciprocity between religion and other cultural values and social behaviour has been a matter of major controversy in sociological and social-anthropological literature. What condition give rise to rationalism and help contiue the traditional way of life is not very much clear. Given the same geographical area and objective conditions what makes a group adopt certain new values while the other group does not ? Even if two groups under similar conditions adopt the same values then what makes them to behave differently ? These problems need to be analysed systematically for the understanding of the relative roles of different institutions in different socio-cultural contexts.

Basing on Max Weber's thesis on Protestant ethics and spirit of capitalism, there are many books and seminars discussing the characteristics of Hindu society, and religion vis-a-vis economic growth and socio-cultural change. The most illuminating debate of recent times is produced by Loomis aud Loomis. But it seems as if a macro analysis of this sort would not help us to come to brass stakes of the problems of the relationship between different institutions. Following Rebert K. Merton it would be better to try to make certain middle range analysis based on empirical studies conducted in middle range socio-cultural system.

Conversion which means a change from one to another. Religious conversion means to change from one religion to another. It may be only for some specific purposes. The convert change his/her name and adopt the way of living of the group mainly structural and partially functional.

In pre-independence days conversions into christianity have take place to a large extent particularly in drought prone areas. Proverty was one of the important factors for these religious conversitions. These conversions were also motivated by the desire to be free from low economic position, illeteracy etc. Many of the Harijans became Christians by the lure of Christian missionaries. In fact, at present conversions from Hinduism to other religions such as Christianity and Islam, were mainly due to poverty. Now a days Christianity relaxed its tenets to some extent and made some concessions such as wearing of 'Tali,' allowing 'bottu,' etc. Generally conversions have taken place among the depressed communities and also economically backward groups particularly among the higher castes groups and the number in the latter case is only very limited.

In Andhra Pradesh there are two major Scheduled Caste groups. They are Malas and Madigas. On a general observation, it seems as though a greater percentage of Malas than the Madigas convert themselves into Christianity and even among the converts the Malas are economically better off than the Madigas. This points to two things—despite more or less the same socio-economic background one group has the propensity to acquire new cultural and religious values and to change their style of life more rapidly than the others. Causes for such differential adoption and change then needed to be looked into in certain structural and historical contexts. This generally tries to investigate such factors.

On a general observation it seems as though the Madigas unlike the Malas, are leather workers, and work under the Jajamani system of rural economy based on Patron-client relationship and are more inter-twined in the village socio-economic structure.

Further, the Malas had, for a long time been, Vaishnavites. This means that probably the Mala group always tried to enhance its social position by way of Sanskritising themselves.

Thus, taking the above two factors into consideration, it seems possible to hypothesise that

(a) these groups which are very much a part of the socio-economic structure of a community have less tendency to change their life than those who are marginal to the given socio-economic system; and

(b) those who have changed their life one, continue to do the same in order to enhance further their position.

Empirical confirmation of these hypothesis with reference to Mala and Madiga Scheduled Caste groups is of great theoretical and practical importance.

Problem

It is quite obvious that even in the traditional organisation the bulk of the Harijans were engaged in the non-defiling occupations. The Harijans including converted Harijans are engaged in the other than polluting occupation of agricultural labour and petty agriculturists whereas Madigas are mainly dependent upon the leather tanning in Konaseema area besides agricultural labour and daily wage earners. The problems of converts were studied at Konaseema as Island surrounded by sea on one side, and the tributories of the river Godavari on the other three sides. This is constituted by 300 villages and in each village there is a considerable percentage of both Malas and Madigas.

This study mainly concentrates on the Harijans and also converted Harijans. In this region, the converted Harijans are structurally Christians but functionally Hindu Harijans. They were converted into Christianity by Christian Missionaries for getting some material benefits but most of them do not have full faith in the Christianity. For all practical purposes they are observing and following Hindu way of life in all spheres. So they remain nominal or Pseudo Christians. The so-called converted Christians like to be called Harijans since they too wish to enjoy all the material and non-material benefits (education, etc.) which their counter parts are enjoying. With them, the rule of the day is reconversion to original group and their craze for identification along with the other Harijans. In the present study, the author mainly paid attention on the converted people whose original caste background is Mala and Madiga. The people of other caste group of Hindu Society who got conversion are not taken into consideration. Hence the term 'converted' means those whose original caste was either Mala or Madiga. Strictly speaking, when once a person is converted, he no longer remains a Hindu but while virtually the converted person not having any implicit faith in the new religion, is emotionally attached to the original religious group and is identified with Mala or Madiga.

Among the Harijans, the marriageable age has now gone up as contrast with that of the previous periods. At present marriages are taking place even after puberty. At present most of the younger generations of both the groups are in favour of inter-caste marriages. The converted Harijans do not have any firm faith pertaining to the Christianity. It is also a pity that even the converted Harijans are subjected to the evil practices of untouchability and hence they are believed by conversion. These converted Harijans by the virtue of their economic or academic status look down upon the people of their original own community as 'untouchables.'

This peculiar custom not only prevails among the converted group but also among the elite group of non converted group. Among the converted, the social status relates to the original background. So that in strict sense they have not been observing Christian rites in mundance activities but for all practical purposes observing Hindu rites in all spheres.

In this region all most all marriages are conducted at the bride's residence. This includes both the converted also. Some of the converted Harijans are celebrating marriage ceremonies according to the ritual processes of Christianity. But these marriages are very limited in number.

Education

Harijans were the most depressed class in education in traditional Hindu Society. They have no opportunity for education. This was one of the factors why other Hindus were able to supress them. Later, the increase in the level of literacy among them can be attributed to some extent to the privileges given to these people and also to the general increase in awareness of the need for education amongst them. The low rates of

Harijan children can be explained in terms of their parents poor economic condition and also ignorance to some extent. In this group most of them have hardly enough to eat. It is unreasonable to expect them to send their children to educational institutions. Every child is considered as an economic asset to the family. The ignorance of the parents and the uncongenial atmosphere in which the child is brought up have deterred the participation of children in education. In this group the elders cannot understand the proper need for education. Added to this, they are also ignorant of what the Government is doing for them.

After the Independence of India, education is spreading rapidly amongst them. It is only due to the introduction of constitutional safeguards and privileges. In view of wide educational facilities, channels are opened for Harijan children. As a result of which every boy goes to school with the exception of a stray case here and there. Further it is pointed out that the converted Harijans rapidly felt the importance of education and hence they are encouraging their children to pursue education better than the Harijans.

By claiming an equal status on par with the other caste Hindus, they at the same time, wish to reap all the benefits approved to them by the Constitution of India. That is how they like to be benefited in both the ways. The converted Harijans are now enmasse trying to get reconverted to their original place in order to claim all advantages like reservations, fee concessions and security of employment, the facilities of which being enjoyed by Harijans. So it clearly indicates that with them religion is only a question of opportunism. In view of the magnanimous tendency of the Government of India towards these Harijans; these converted Harijans are happening to get reconverted to enjoy these delicious fruits and facilities. They say that they got converted to Christianity once to cast off the social stigma of untouchability and to receive monetary benefits rendered directly by Christian Missionaries, or some times through Christian agents. At present they want to be back to the original fold simply because there is no any type in the Christian religion nor incentives from the Christian Missionaries and they run to that place where there is attraction.

Economic Organisation

The study of economic organisation is as important as that of the other institutions like religious, political and social. It is not only the maintainer but also regulator of different aspects of life. This explains why it is commonly mentioned that one who is economically dependent cannot but be dependent in all other spheres.

The major occupation of the Harijans is agriculture and agricultural labour. Every ryot cultivating paddy has an attached labourer from a Harijan family. For example, watering the fields and guarding the fields from stray cattle are two important tasks. Besides, a wide variety of services extracted from the Harijan labourer. They have to work in the agricultural fields or in some cases to look after the live stock and engage themselves throughout the day. Traditionally Harijans are mainly a labouring group.

Deviation from the traditional occupation may mean change in the standard of living; change in the structure and function of the organisation of that group. Need for a better standard of living is effected mainly because of changes in outlook and values—New opportunities in employment resulting from the influx of science and technology and opportunities in the acquisition of education and a new type of livelihood. It is because of the changing socio-economic means in these people which have been instrumental in introducing mobility in all circles and change. Now-a-days this change is predominantly seen among the Scheduled Castes. Most of the Harijans are comparatively mall in number to that of the converted regarding skilled works. Several factors have contributed to the advancement of the converted Harijans. For instance improvement in education, awareness of socio-political changes and also adopting the ways and life of the high caste people (Process of Sanskritization). With all these, the converted Harijans are far better than the non-converted. The same kind of results are also observed in the group of semi-skilled. Whereas in the case of non-skilled work, the Harijans are seen more in number in this type than that of the converted in the region of Konaseema in Andhra Pradesh.

As mentionad earlier, agriculture is the main traditional occupation. Two natural factors are of primary importance for a successful agrarian economy in Konaseema are–Soil and climatic conditions. The climate includes temperature—rainfall and also irrigation facilities in the region—Naturally the relationship of people to land which has a vital bearing on agrarian economy, the unit of production in this field area among Harijans are based on individual possession of cultivable land. Because of the patriarchal society, the land is normally transmitted from father to male children and all the vested interests are in the hands of the head of the family. Suppose if a joint family breaks up, automatically the land is divided equally amongst the male children and finally becomes small land holdings.

Religious Organisation

Both Harijans and converted have firm faith in religious beliefs and practices. In Konaseema area Harijans are worshipping the deities associated with great and little traditional levels. Also they worship the deities of the All India Phenomenon as well as regional and local deities. Besides these, they celebrate some of the Jatharas in honour of the deities such as Mutyalamm, Matamma, Gotelamma, Gouramma etc. during crisis periods.

Both Harijans and converted to Jagaranas and observing fastings on some important days such as Mahashivaratri and Vaikunta Ekadasi in order to attain moksha (Salvation).

While pointing out the Psychological set up of the Harijans in Konaseema area—regarding the term Harijans and the reconversion of the converted from Christianity to Hindu religion one cannot but feel it quite interesting. In reality the Harijans discarding Christian religion and retaining their original identify i.e. as Hindu. They wish to consider themselves as Malas or Madigas or Harijans and the same was extended to converted.

The practice of untouchability is on the swinging line. It is not so seriously observed as in the past particularly in rural parts. In a nut shell, this untouchability, which is being dinner into the ears of people as anti-national, in human and indescent. The converted who want to escape this social stigma embarassed Christianity, faced all humiliation on par with their counter parts despite their conversion. At present the untouchability is slowly wanning from the scene, and Harijans including converted feel happy to have overcome this evil. They also reap all the benefits along with their counter-parts, they are enmasse getting reconversion into Hindu religion.

The economic position of Malas is good and are better placed that Madigas. Most of them are still observing the traditional occupation. A good noticeable number were engaged in new occupations, other than the traditional occupations because of changes in values and in outlook governing the style of life, new opportunities in occupations resulting from the influx of science and technology, and also better opportunities in the acquisition of new sources of livelihood. It is because of the changing socio-economic conditions in India which have been instrumental in introducing occupational movement and change in the system. This change is generally seen among the artisan castes and lower caste groups and particularly among the Harijans including converted.

In reality after the Independence there has been a movement among the Malas towards christianity. These converts are enumerated as Christians and are not included among the Malas. In this Konaseema area, the influence of Christianity on these two groups in quite remarkable and a considerable number among Malas and Madigas have been converted by the Christian Missionaries.

Now-a-days the needs of Harijans are not many. They need for to some extent—socio-economic, political, educational and employment concerns in order to cover their deficiency and become self-sufficient and also expect equality with other sections of human society and human treatment in Hindu India.

It is understand that the Muslim and other Christian countries such as the Gulf and United States have agents in India and are working out with the people such as the economically weaker sections, the backward class, the Scheduled Caste and Tribal people by tipping off them with money for their conversion into the respective religions. If such act continue for a few decades, the forward caste people Hindus will become the minority people and the Indian country will be dominated and controlled by these converts.

References

1. Bala Surya Prasad Bhopal, "*Andhra Vijnanam,*" *Telugu Encyclopedia* printed by Rajan Electrical Press, Rajahmundry.
2. Briggs Geo. W., "*The Chamars,*" B. R. Publishing Corporation, Delhi-110052.
3. Desai I.P., "*Untouchabilities in Rural Gujarat,*" Popular Prakashan, Bombay-400034.
4. Moorthy B.S., "*Depressed and Oppressed,*" S. Chand & Co, (Pvt) Limited, Ram Nagar, New Delhi.

5. Ramesh Thaper (Ed.,) 1977, *Tribe, Caste and Religion in India*, "The Problem of Untouchables" by Roy Burmon.
6. Robert K. Merton, "*Social Theory and Social Structure*," The Free Press, New York Collier Machavillian Limited, London.
7. Singe T.R., "*The Madigas*"—Ethnographic and Polk Culture Society, Lucknow, U.P.
8. Srinivas M.N., "*Social Change in Modern India*," University of California Press, Berkeley & Los. Angles, 1967.
9. Sachidananda, "*The Harijan Elite*," Thomas Press (India) Limited, 1977.
10. Stephen Fuchs, "*Children of Hari*," New Order Book Company, Ahmedabad.
11. Sunanda Patwardhan, "*Change Among Indias' Harijans*," Oriental Longman Limited, 315 Asaf Ali Road, New Delhi-110001.
12. Thurston Edgar, "*Castes and Tribes of Southern India*," Cosmo Publications, 24-B, New Delhi-110006.
13. Trivedi H.R., *Scheduled Caste Woman Studies in Exploitation*," Concept Publishing Company, Delhi.
14. L.P. Vdyarthi, "*Harijan Today*."

TEN

The Continuity of Disabilities of Scheduled Castes in India

Dr. S.M. Dahiwale

The post-Independent SCs were known by a variety of terms at different times. During the Vedic age the present-day Scheduled Castes people were included in the category of Shudra. It is clear from a mention what Atri declared a washerman, a leather-worker, a cane worker, a fisherman, and a Bhil as Antyajas or outcastes (Ghurye : 1969; 98). In traditional India the untouchables were known as the 'antyas' or 'bahyas' people living outside villages and towns (Sharma : 195 8; 130) The British Government identified them as 'untouchables,' 'depressed classes' and 'Scheduled Castes' at different times. Since the Vedic age to the present-day post-Independent India, a Hindu Society has a history of SCs of their disabilities. Here the changing nature of their disabilities has been delineated.

I

Disabilities of Shudras in an Ancient India

An account of religious, economic and civil disabilities, and also the severity of punishment to the Shudras has been sketched below :

A. Religious Disabilities

A number of religious disabilities were imposed on Shudras. They were allowed to use the current exclamation namah (Ghurye : *Op. cit.* ; 122). They were not to be admitted to the Upanayana and the study of the Veda (*Ibid.*, 119). Neither they were allowed to listen to or recite the Vedic hymns. Also, they were not allowed to follow the Ashram system (Buhler : 1972; 229). If a Shudra recited Vedas his tongue was cut off. It is because they were regarded unfit for twice born and so they had no right to wear the sacred thread and also they were made disqualified to receive religious blessings. Shudras were not admitted to the ceremony of sacrifice. Dutt elaborated that; 'though the Shudra was present at the Ashwamegha sacrifice in the capacity of a watchman, the privilege of abhishekh (ritual sprinkling) was not given to him and he was not to be admitted to the hall of sacrifice. He was also deprived of the right of initiation and the right of drinking soma at sacrifices' (Dutt : 1968; 87-88). They were not allowed to milk for fire-oblation) (Ghurye : *Op. cit.*; 51). A marriage of Shudra was also not regarded as sacrament but was regarded only as a sexual union (*Ibid.* ; 60-61). Shudras were prohibited from practising austerities. In this regard, a story of the Ramayana is quoted that Rama had killed a Shudra for practising austerities (*Ibid.*; 60). It is well-known fact that the temples built by the labour of Shudras were not open for them. Similarly, a Shudra could not attain individual salvation after death, which was a privilege to other three Varnas. Thus, a Shudra was unfit for initiating a ceremony of twice-born, for studying Vedas or reciting the Vedic hymns, for performing a sacrifice, for offering fire-oblations and for practising austirities.

B. Economic Deprivation

According to the Mahabharata the Shudras can have no right to own property (*Ibid.*; 61). He was not permitted to acquire wealth (*Ibid.*; 91). Kautilya mentioned regarding the means of livelihood of Shudras. They had two sources of livelihood, i.e., service of twice-born castes and their own professions *viz.*, artisans, dancers, actors etc. (Sharma : *Op cit.*; 146). Shudras were always associated with the removal, street sweeping and cremation of corpses (*Ibid.*; 127). The duty was imposed on them to pick up and carry the dead bodies of animals and human beings. They were employed as agricultural labourers and slaves (*Ibid.*; 149). Dutt remarked that the professions of 'Sudras were regarded as impure and they were degraded to the level of the slave (Dutt ; *Op. cit.*; 23 & Ghurye : *Op. cit.*; 50). Also, the outcastes persons were deprived of the occupations of the twice-born (Ghurye : *Op. cit.*; 55). The food and clothes remnants and castaways by the three Varnas were the sources of support for survival to the Shudras (*Ibid.*; 59). Thus it is clear that the Shudras' economic life was degraded to the lowest position.

C. Disabilities in Civil Life

A Shudra had no right of sitting, conversing, or going along the road with twice-born men and if he does so he should receive corporal punishment (*Ibid.*; 62). It is quoted that if a Shudra commits adultery with woman of the twice-born, he shall suffer capital punishment (*Ibid.*). Various prohibitions against a Shudra were to be observed by a twice-born person *viz.*, not to go on journey in the company of a Shudra, not to eat food or accept water given by a Shudra, not to marry a Shudra female by a Brahmin, not to express sentiments of compassion about a Shudra and so on (*Ibid.*). The Chandals were treated as untouchables (*Ibid*; 79) Manu declared them to be worthy of being settled outside the town-limits (*Ibid.*; 97). Ghurye quoted that the objects like vehicles and seats defiled by the touch of a Shudra were to be rendered unfit for use unless water was sprinkled over them (*Ibid.*). That is to say that the position of Shudras in ancient India was degraded down to the animals.

D. Severe Punishments to the Shudras

In Manusmriti Shudras have been discriminated against for punishment. A severe punishment is laid down to the Shudras on the violation of the rules of the Shastra. For abusing a member of the Dwija caste the Shudra's tongue was to be mutilated. In case a Shudra abused a Brahmin by using his name he was punished by inserting in his mouth a red hot iron bar. For preaching a Brahmin a Sudra was punishable with pouring burning oil down his throat and ears. It is pointed out that the most severe punishment was to be awarded to a Shudra and the least to a Brahmin (Tiwari : 1963; 61). In this way the Shudras were not only discriminated against in the matter of punishments but also they were severely punished.

II

Social Disabilities during the Maratha Period

During the Maratha period (1600-1818 A.D.) in Maratha country, i.e., the present Western Maharashtra the traditional order of the Hindu society seems to be unchanged. A sovereign Maratha kingdom is identified from the emergence of Shivaji Chhatrapati. King Shivaji made clear his policy towards the various castes in his Royal Order issued on January 28, 1677 AD that : "The practices of each caste as handed down by tradition should be scrupulously observed" (See Bhavare's art. in Kamble : 1982; 187-88). And King Shivaji preserved the system of Chaturvarnya without disturbing the framework of society during his rule.

During the Peshwa period i.e., the 18th century a number of interdictions were imposed on the members of each caste regarding marriage, dining, drinking and social contact (Gawali: 1988; 16). In Maharashtra the Balutedari system is known for its village economy. The essential feature of the system is that the artisan castes and the other untouchable castes had to provide services essentially or occasionally to village people (*Ibid.*; 22-23). In the system, especially the position of the Mahar was as bad as a slave. It is because a Mahar had to perform a number of duties (*Ibid.*; 132-54). It is mentioned that under the Peshwas the Mahars, the Mangs and the Chambhars were untouchables and also they were living outside the village (*Ibid.*; 130-31). Regarding the interrelationship certain strict rules were imposed on the members of each caste. The Brahmin was not permitted to employ a woman as a maid-servant from the untouchable castes i.e., Mahar of Chambhar (*Ibid.*; 132). Some mentions are on the historical documents that the upper caste-Hindu men were not permitted to have illicit intercourse with a Mahar or Mang woman and the identified upper caste-Hindu men were to be excommunicated (*Ibid*), and when a lowest Mang had intercourse with a upper caste-Hindu woman he was to be murdered (*Ibid.*; 143). In case of crimes such as theft, robbery and dacoity severe punishment (i.e., beheading, cutting off ear, hand and leg) was awarded to Mahar criminals (*Ibid.*; 135-36). A practice of forced labour was prevalent and the Mahars, the Mangs and the Chambhars were employed towards it (*Ibid.*; 136-37). The lower castes were forbidden certain usages and customs e.g., doning the sacred thread etc., practised by the Brahmins (*Ibid.*; 143). An untouchable girl, a student of Mahatma Phule's school of the 19th century has stated in her essay, that 'it was not possible to the Mahars and Mangs to pass through the roads of Peshwa's palace in Pune city' (Joshi : 1971; 163). From the above account it is clear that the position of the members of the untouchable castes was degraded below the level of the animal.

III

Disabilities of Untouchables during the British Period

Till pre-British regime the supremacy of the Brahmins and their authority over the Shastras was neither disturbed nor challenged. The Hindu kings also restored the order of the Hindu social structure and system. But, with the advent of the British a number of new systems emerged and developed, viz., a Government of modern legislations, a modern bureaucracy and administration, new means of communication such as posts and mass media, a system of modern formal education based on scientific and rational temper, the growth of industries in cities and its large-scale organizations and a number of Christian missionaries to the educational and medical services of the poor In spite of these many new things, a Hindu society remained unchanged. The important thing which is to be noted here is that, at the initial stage the British Government had adopted the policy of non-interference in the internal affairs of the Hindus' religion and customs. Nevertheless, the new systems in the British rule affected the traditional institutions of the Hindu society with certain limitations. It was not possible to change the entire order of Hindu society at once. Therefore, we come across with a number of complaints regarding disabilities suffered by those untouchables of the British India.

In the Maratha country the various duties of the village which were imposed on the Mahars continued even during the British period. In the Bombay Presidency of the British India the Mahars had to perform a number of duties as inferior hereditary officers to the various Government departments *viz.*, irrigation, revenue, education, police and local self government. The Mahars were to be called upon to render their services at any time of day and night. In return to their services they had two sources of livelihood i.e., a piece of inam land and the baluta (grains from the peasants) (Government of Maharashtra : 1982; 74-77). That is why Dr. Babasaheb Ambedkar described the Watan system as an atrocious and barbarious system (*Ibid.*; 84). An incident is mentioned that, one Mahar with socks and boots was not allowed to enter the main village and also the act of putting tiles by a Mahar on his house was not tolerated by the caste Hindus, and those who did so against the practice a social boycott against the community was declared (*Ibid.*; 79). A case is reported that till 1926 a Bhangi (sweeper) was not allowed to board a tram in Bombay city (*Ibid.* : 482).

The untouchables were not admitted to the public places such as watering places, wells and dharamshalas. It is evidenced from the resolution passed in the Bombay Legislative Council (*Ibid.*; 279). A case is mentioned that in the year 1856 a Mahar boy was denied admission to the Dharwar Government School (*Ibid.*; 418). In many schools the Mahar boys were not allowed to enter the classroom but they had to sit at Varandah (Ghurye: *Op. cit.*, 275). It is mentioned that in the year 1927 in the city of Bombay, the depressed class children were given separate pots for drinking water (Government of Maharashtra: *Op. cit.*; 457). The doors of the Hindu temples were closed to the untouchables is a widely known fact. The famous temple entry agitations which were led (consequently those went failure) under the leadership of untouchables at Nasik, Amravati and Poona in Maharashtra, and also under the leadership of Mahatma Gandhi at Guruvayur in Kerala are the sufficient examples to suggest that the untouchables had to suffer from such disability. In the year 1929 Dr. Ambedkar had given an account of the socio-economic disabilites of the untouchables of the times, that :

> Untouchables could not enter the Police, the Army and the Navy as their touch was causing pollution, the professions like trade and industry were closed to them, they were not free to dress and live as they liked, they might not wear better clothes than the high caste-Hindus, they had to live in hut, and could not take the bridegroom on a horse in procession through the main streets of the village, if an untouchable was a victim of the majority tyranny the Police hardly was to come to his rescue (*Ibid.*; 358).

It is mentioned that in the year 1927 a medical practitioner not only refused to enter the untouchable's quarters but he refused to see the patient and to apply the thermometer also (*Ibid.*; 450). The complaint was reported in the year 1928 that the High case-Hindus of some villages in Indore district had framed certain rules against the Balais. The rules imposed were :

1. Balais must not wear gold lace and bordered pugrees.
2. They must not wear dhoties with coloured or fancy borders.
3. They must convey intimation of the death of any Hindu to relatives of deceased—no matter how far away the relatives stayed.
4. In all Hindu marriages, the Balais must play, music before the processions, and during the marriages.
5. The Balai women must not wear gold or silver ornaments; they must not wear fancy gowns, or jackets.
6. Balai women must attend all cases of confinement of Hindu women.
7. The Balais must render services without demanding remuneration, and must accept whatever a Hindu is pleased to give.
8. If the Balais do not agree to abide by these terms, they must clear out of the villages (*Ibid.*; 452). This example is sufficient to indicate the caste tyranny.

It is mentioned that it was not possible to invite a respectable untouchable to a house of caste Hindu, and in case it is done the caste council would not only condemn him but also would pass a judgement against the householder as unfit for social intercourse (Ghurye : *Op. cit.*; 282). An incident of some villages in Solapur district was reported that the effort of the Mahars of giving up of the carrying of the carcasses of dead animals at self-improvement was not tolerated by the caste-Hindus and in consequence the villagers had declared the economic boycott (Government of Maharashtra : *Op. cit.*; 281).

IV

Practice of Untouchability, Atrocities etc. on SCs during the Post-Independent India

During the post-Independent period in spite of the Constitutional and Statutory measures and also making the practice of untouchability punhishable under the Protection of Civil Rights Act the condition of SCs has not improved and the disabilities on the grounds of untouchability continued adding incidents of complaints regarding the practice of untouchability, harassments, torture, atrocities and tyranny. The account of their social, economic and educational sufferings is stated below.

A. Observance of Untouchability

A number of Reports of the Commissioner for SCs and STs (Govt. of India : 1959; 32-37, 49 & 50, 1960, 29-31 1962; 27-30 & 42-44, 1963; 6, 1964; 7 & 8, 1965; 14, 15, 18 & 19, 1965; 15-23 & 26, 1967; 14-21 & 25, 1967; 83-91 & 93-96, 1977; 103-104, 1980; 181-191, and 1982; 209-228) inform us regarding the prevalence of the practice of untouchability. There are some common forms of untouchability which are being observed not only in villages but in towns and cities also. In many parts of the country untouchability has been rigidly observed against the Bhangis or the Mehtars in towns and cities as well. Generally the high caste persons neither receive nor eat cooked food given by the persons from the lowest caste groups. In many parts of village India, the village wells are not open to SCs. They are not allowed to use hand pumps constructed in many villages. It has been the common experience to the SC persons that they have been denied rented accommodation not only in villages but in cities also. The barbers and the washermen refuse services to the lowest castes on the grounds of untouchability. In Rajasthan the SC persons had no access to inns. The lowest ex-untouchables were not allowed to sit on the same cot with high caste persons or in presence of the high caste Hindus.

In some parts of India the lowest ex-untouchables could not ride a horse. As stated in the Fourteenth Report of the Commissioner for SCs/STs (1964 65) in some areas of Tamil Nadu the SCs were not allowed to carry dead bodies, to wear shoes, to ride on cycles through the localities of caste Hindus. In an area of Union Territory of Delhi the lowest castes were prevented from using public roads. In some villages the entry in hotel was barred. In some places tea was served outside the hotel or in separate tumblers or coconut shell kept outside the stalls and also water was poured from a distance. Whenever the lowest caste persons were invited to the house of higher caste on occasions they were made to sit separately. As stated in the Twelfth Report of the Commissioner for SCs/STs (1962-63), the survey observed discrimination against SCs in Gujarat State that, the SCs had to wash their clothes or take bath at separate ghats of the tanks and also they were compelled to use the river-water down stream only. Further it is reported that separate drinking water arrangements were made for SC employees in the Municipal and Grampanchayat offices. And separate burial or cremation grounds existed for the SCs. In some villages of Gujarat, the SCs were served clothes, flour, sweetmeat and grocery from a distance by the caste-Hindu shop owners.

According to the Eleventh Report of the Commissioner for SCs/STs (1961-62) in some of the villages of Madhya Pradesh the ex-untouchable persons were not allowed to put on a turban with turrha. In some villages marriage processions were not allowed to pass through the localities of high caste Hindus. In some parts of India a music-band was not allowed to play at the marriage. And the women were not permitted to wear ornaments made of silver. The ex-untouchables were neither allowed to enter temples nor were allowed to offer sweets or flowers to the deity. In Mathura-Varindavan if an ex-untouchable disclosed his identity he was not allowed to enter the temple. In some villages of Bihar the SCs were not allowed to attend the Kirtan. The same Report stated that in some interior villages the ex-untouchable pupils had to sit separately. Also, in some schools they were not allowed to touch the bucket, glass or lota kept there. In some villages the high caste-Hindus did not allow the ex-untouchable children to join the schools. In the University of Allahabad the SC IAS trainees were refused tea by the manager of the canteen.

In the Fourteenth Report of the Commissioner SCs/STs (1964-65) it is stated that in a village of Gujarat a SC teacher was not allowed to enter the store-room of the school. In some hostels attached to Government schools and colleges of Jammu and Kashmir State the SC students were discriminated against in common rooms and kitchens. In some cases the higher officers have used disrespectful and objectionable language against SCs and also insulted them. It has been reported that in some village Panchayats the SCs were not allowed to sit on chairs. In village of Gujarat in the year 1977, the caste Hindus did not allow to enrol the ex-untouchables of the village as members of the village Milk Cooperative Society.

According to the Twenty-sixth Report of the Commissioner for SCs/STs (1978-79) the ex-untouchables were assaulted and insulted while taking seat in a bus or by chance touching caste-Hindus or their vessels, and such cases were reported from the state of Gujarat, Haryana, Kerala, Pondicherry, Madhya Pradesh, and Uttar Pradesh (pp. 190-91). The extent of untouchability can easily be understood as the number of registered cases under the Protection of Civil Rights Act, 1955 has increased in the country from 526 in 1971 (Govt. of India : 1977; 103) to 4087 in 1982 (Govt. of India; 1985; 114).

B. Cases of Atrocities, Harassments, Torture and Insults

Day by day incidents of atrocities on SCs are increasing. The figures show that the atrocity cases during the year 1979 were 13,975 in number which rose to 15,054 in 1982 (*Ibid.*; 118). A variety of forms of atrocities were committed such as murder, rape, molestation of women, illegal dispossession of land of SCs, burning alive (as occurred at Belchi, a village in Bihar and also at many other places), violence resulting in grievous hurt, arson, burning of houses, preventing from cultivation of land and harvesting of crops, unlawful eviction from the land in possession and the like (*Ibid.*; 120, 122 & 124). And the causes of atrocities have been reported that of social awakening and assertion by the SCs on account of problems relating to the practice of untouchability, harassment, land disputes, housing, non-payment of minimum wages, forced labour, refusal to carry out the traditional caste duties etc. (*Ibid.*; 1977; 107-112, 1980; 73-115 & 230-257, 1981; 314-355, 1982; 147-157, 340-344 & 354-378).

A number of complaints have been reported relating to the denial of justice to SC employees in service matters (*Ibid.*; 1982; 88-95). The cases of harassments of SC persons were reported not only from the offices but also from the experiences of varied interactional levels with the caste Hindus. A variety of cases of complaints of harassments, tortures, insults were reported such as insulting by using caste name, commenting on the colour of the skin, depriving from opportunity to appear at the examination or depriving from confirmation and promotion chances in the service, not relieving for training, not forwarding the application for other or higher post, not considering for appointment under this or that pretext, not issuing caste certificates to SC applicants by the Pradhans of Gram Panchayats and as such (*Ibid.*; 1967; 85-90 & 1982; 281-296).

C. *Economic Disabilities*

The phenomenon of poverty in India is comprehended on economic criteria. The Plan document mentioned the number of poor but the percentage of poor among the SCs is not separately shown. However, the Govt. documents admitted that the bulk of SCs was among the poorest of the population (*Ibid.*; 1982; 3 & 1984; 23). But the figure 76.39% of the SC population indicated as cultivators and agricultural labourers (*Ibid.*; 1985; 47) reveals that their larger population belongs to the group of poor. The prevalence of bonded labour among the SC population can be considered for identification of poverty among them. In spite of the enactment in the year 1976 of the Central Law abolishing bonded labour and the new 20-Point Programme as well, the Reports of the Commissioner for SCs/STs inform us that the bonded labourers were identified mostly from the SCs (*Ibid.*; 1977; 28 & 30, 1980; 22—29, 1982; 33 & 35). And the prevalence of bonded labour was attributed to indebtedness as a major cause. However, the Fifth Report of the Commissioner for SCs/STs informed that 80% of the bonded labourers who were identified in the country belonged to SCs and STs (*Ibid.*; 1985; 112).

So far as the adoption of modern jobs is concerned a little progress has been revealed among some caste groups of untouchable category (See Parmar : 1978; 228-237, Saberwal ; 1973; 234-259, Patwardhan : 1973; 203, Gangarde : 1975; 252, Deasi : 1976; 162, Gare & Limaye 1970, Kulkarni & Hiramani : 1975; 96-97, Doshi : 1980, Mehra *et. al.* : 1984; 335, Lapoint & Lapoint : 1985, Rahate : 1985; 188, Santhakumari & Dahiwale : 1989). Some recent studies, however, observed that the Bhangis were still in their caste-jobs of scavenging (Sarkar : 1984; 71 & Shyamlal : 1984; 32-39).

Further it is interesting to know the share of SC households in the ownership of land among the total households in rural areas of the country. In this regard the Thirty-seventh NSS round has revealed that the SC households constituting 19.71% of total households had a share of only 7.89% which was the lowest in the total ownership of land holdings (Govt. of India : 37th NSS Round; 1987, 30).

Thus in spite of the various welfare programmes of the Government the economic condition of a majority of SCs/STs is still pathetic.

D. Educational Development

Despite the special educational facilities and anti-disabilities measures for SCs, the literacy rate in the year 1981 for SCs was only 21.38% against 36.17% at All-India level (*Ibid.*; 1985; 95). The percentage of enrolment of SCs to total enrolment at High/Higher Secondary stage during the year 1978-79 at All-India level was 9.9 (*Ibid.*; 1982; 305). These figures reveal a wide gap when compared with the enrolment of caste-Hindus to the enrolment of SCs. Despite reservation and other educational facilities many seats were not filled up by SC candidates in professional colleges, in Central institutions and at under-graduate and post-graduate levels (*Ibid.*; 103-05). Thus the poor progress of SCs in education is alone of the indicators for their overall backwardness.

The policy of reservation is enshrined in Articles 16 (4) and 335 of the Constitution but during the recent years the caste-Hindus have expressed their resentment over it and so an organized anti-reservation widespread agitation led by the caste-Hindus in Gujarat in the year 1981 is an example before all of us. Apart from the people's opposition in general, there are examples of non-SC/ST employees who had opposed reservation of vacancies on promotion (*Ibid.*; 1982; 57). Despite the reservation measures for employment opportunities in India 16,61,081 educated Scheduled Caste job-seekers were on the liveregister as on 31.12.1979 (*Ibid.*; 15). The figure is indicative of the society of the problem of unemployment among the educated Scheduled Castes. However, the percentages of SC employees in various services show the slight progress (*Ibid.*; 1985; 130-173). But it indicates for their marginal representation in the service sector of the country.

In this way the educational progress and a representation in services of the SCs/STs appear to be poor.

Summary

The present SCs were/are regarded as untouchables. They had to suffer from a number of disabilities such as religious, economic, civil etc. In ancient India a number of disabilities were imposed on Shudras. They were regarded unfit for admission to the ceremony of sacrifice and for the salvation. The Shudras had no right to own property but they had to attend to the services of the twice-born castes. Regarding social intercourse a Shudra had to observe the distance, because by his touch the twice-born person was to be polluted. So far as the punishment is concerned a Shudra was discriminated against by more severe punishment.

During the Maratha period (especially in Western Maharashtra) the order of the Hindu society did not change. And especially during the Peshwa period a number of interdictions were imposed on the untouchables. The position of Mahar was as bad as slave. The practice of forced labour was prevalent and mostly the untouchables were employed. In general, the life of the untouchable was worse than animal.

During the British period a little improvement was seen in the position of untouchable. However, it has not been possible to change the traditional order of the society. A noteworthy fact is that during the British period a resistence had been registered by the members of the untouchable castes. As a result of some progressive legislations the untouchables have led movements to exercise their civil rights, for example, entering the temples at Nasik, Amravati and Pune and also at Mahad for using water of the *Chavadar Tale*.

During the post-Independent period a number of cases were reported regarding the observance of untouchability under the Protection of Civil Rights Act, 1955. The incidents of atrocities on SCs have risen to 15,054 in the year 1982. In spite of the various Governmental measures the bulk of the SCs is found among the poorest of the population. The practice of bonded labour is abolished by the law of 1976 but the bonded labourers were identified mostly from the SCs. Although the process of modernization and industrialization has taken place, a majority of SC population is still engaged in their caste and the lower rungs of the occupations. Moreover, a very noteworthy feature is that despite the land legislations, according to the 37th NSS Report, the SCs have the lowest share i.e., 7.89% in the total ownership of land holdings. Regarding the literacy level of SCs, according to the 1981 census it is only 21.38% against 36.17% at All-India level. Although a number of educational and reservation facilities have been provided to the number of SCs, many seats in professional/career institutions, and in Government and non-Government offices have not been filled up. Thus the picture is clear of their poor progress in the fields of education, modern occupation and service.

Concluding Remarks

It means the process of industrialization, urbanization and modernization, and the legeal measures adopted during the post-Independent period in the interests of the SCs proved to be of little help in improving the social, economic, educational and cultural conditions of those SCs. What is more important is the need to bring about a change in the attitude of the caste-Hindus and secondly, the need of honest and sincere initiative from the section of SCs itself. The attitude of dependence which persists among them since centuries must be overcome to keep pace with their caste-Hindu counterparts.

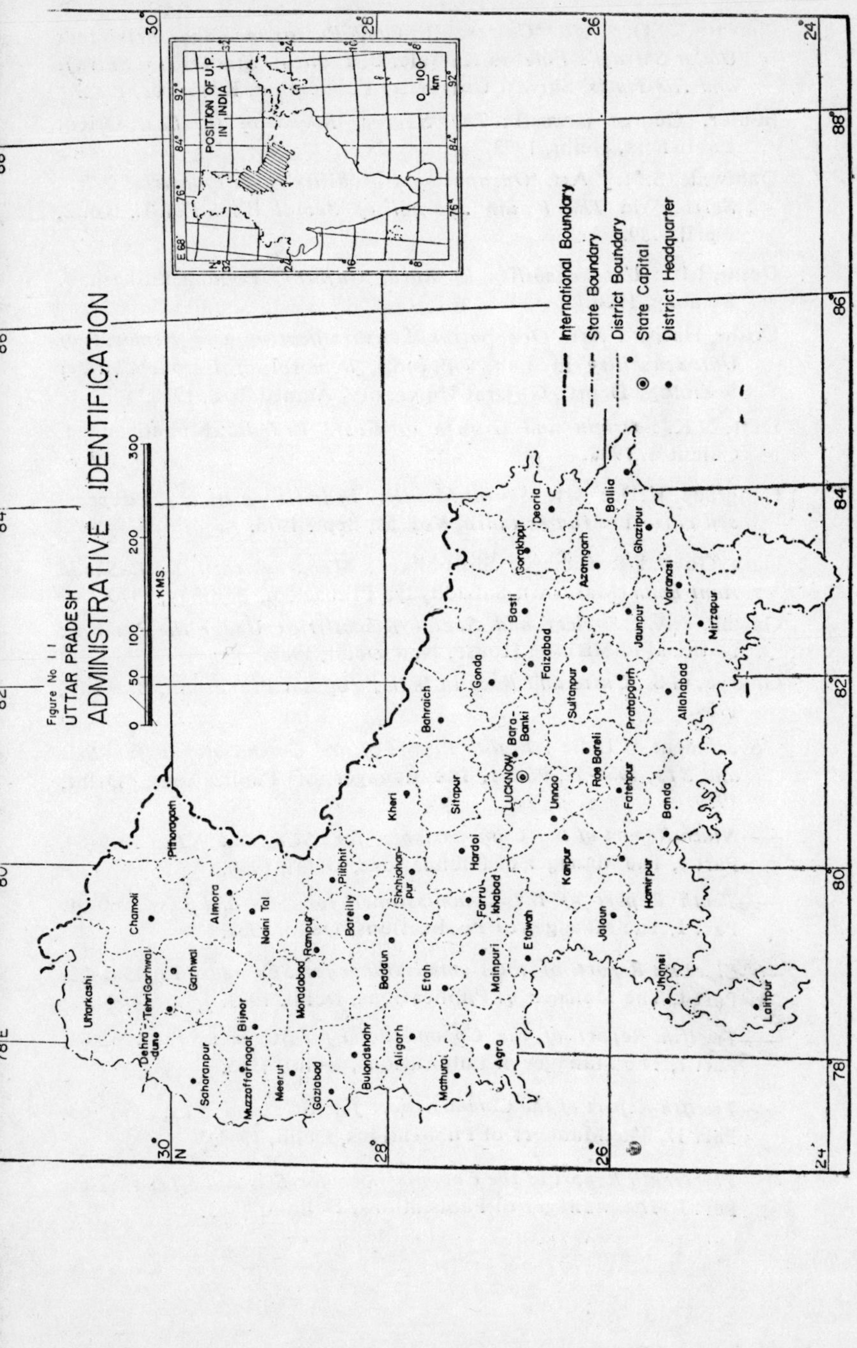
Figure No 1.1
UTTAR PRADESH
ADMINISTRATIVE IDENTIFICATION
0 50 100 200 300
KMS.
POSITION OF U.P. IN INDIA
International Boundary
State Boundary
District Boundary
State Capital
District Headquarter
Uttarkashi
Chamoli
Pithoragarh
Tehri Garhwal
Garhwal
Almora
Naini Tal
Dehra dune
Saharanpur
Muzaffarnagar
Bijnor
Meerut
Moradabad
Rampur
Gaziabad
Bulandshahr
Badaun
Bareilly
Pilibhit
Aligarh
Etah
Shahjahanpur
Kheri
Mathura
Agra
Mainpuri
Farrukhabad
Hardoi
Sitapur
Bahraich
Etawah
Kanpur
Unnao
LUCKNOW
Bara-Banki
Gonda
Basti
Gorakhpur
Deoria
Faizabad
Sultanpur
Azamgarh
Ballia
Ghazipur
Jaunpur
Varanasi
Mirzapur
Allahabad
Pratapgarh
Rae Bareli
Fatehpur
Banda
Hamirpur
Jalaun
Jhansi
Lalitpur

References

Bhavare, N.G. : Art. '*Castes, Favours, Patronage and Privileges Under Shivaji's Rule*' in Kamble, B.R. (ed.); *Studies in Shivaji and His Times*, Shivaji University Publication, Kolhapur, 1982.

Buhler, George (trans.) : *The Sacred Books of the East*; Orient Publishers, Delhi, 1972.

Dahiwale, S.M. : Art. '*Occupational Mobility in an Industrial Urban Setting*' in *The Indian Journal of Social Work Vol.* L, No. 2, April 1989.

Desai, I.P. : *Untouchability in Rural Gujarat*; Popular Prakashan, Bombay, 1976.

Doshi, Harish : Art. '*Occupational Diversification and Removal of Untouchability*' in Shah, V.P. (ed); *Removal of Untouchability*; Sociology Deptt , Gujarat University, Ahmedabad, 1980.

Dutt, N.K. : *Origin and Growth of Caste in India*; Mukhopadhya, Calcutta, 1968.

Gangrade, K.D. : Art. '*Social Mobility in India—a study of depressed class*' in *Man in India*, Vol. 55, Sept. 1975.

Gare, Govind & Limaye, Shirubhau : *Maharashtratil Dalit-Shodh Aani Bodh* (Marathi); Sahadhyaya Prakashan, Bombay, 1970.

Gawali, P.A. : *Society and Social Disabilities Under the Peshwas*; National Publishing House, New Delhi, 1988.

Ghurye, G.S.: *Caste and Race in India*; Popular Prakashan, Bombay, 1969.

Government of India : *Eighth Report of the Commissioner for SCs and STs*; 1958-59, Part I, The Manager of Publications, Delhi, 1959.

——*Ninth Report of the Commissioner for SCs and STs*; 1959-60, Part I, The Manager of Publications, Delhi, 1960.

——*Tenth Report of the Commissioner for SCs and STs*; 1960-61, Part I, The Manager of Publications, Delhi, 1962.

——*Eleventh Report of the Commissioner for SCs and STs*; 1961-62, Part I, The Manager of Publications, Delhi, 1963.

——*Twelfth Report of the Commissioner for SCs and STs*; 1962-63, Part I, The Manager of Publications, Delhi, 1965.

——*Twelfth Report of the Commissioner for SCs and STs*; 1962-63, Part II, The Manager of Publications, Delhi, 1964.

——*Thirteenth Report of the Commissioner for SCs and STs*; 1963-64, Part I, The Manager of Publications, Delhi-6, 1965.

Government of India : *Fourteenth Report of the Commissioner for SCs and STs*; 1964-65 The Manager of Publications, Delhi, 1967.

——*Fourteenth Report of the Commissioner for SCs and STs*; 1965-66, Vols. I & II, The Manager of Publications, Delhi, 1967.

——*Twentyfourth Report of the Commissioner for SCs and STs*; 1975-76 and 1976-77, Part I, The Manager of Publications, New Delhi.110002, 1977.

——*Twenty-sixth Report of the Commissioner for SCs and STs*; 1978-79, 1980.

——*Twenty-seventh Report of the Commissioner for SCs and STs*, 1979-81, Part I, The Controller of Publications, Delhi-110054, 1982.

——*Twenty-seventh Report of the Commissioner for SCs and STs*, 1979-81, Part II, (Appendices), The Controller of Publications, Delhi-110054, 1982.

——*Report of the Commissioner for* SCs *and STs*, July 1978, March 1979, The Controller of Publications, Delhi-110054, 1980.

——*Report of the Commissioner for SCs and STs*, April 1979, March 1980, The Controller of Publications, Delhi-110054, 1981.

——*Report of the Commissioner for SCs and STs*; April 1981-March 1982 (Fourth Report), The Controller of Publications, Delhi-54, 1984.

——*Report of the Commissioner for SCs and STs*; April 1982-March 198‹ (Fifth Report), The Controller of Publications, Delhi-54, 1985.

——*Thirtyseventh NSS Round*; *January December 1982*, National Sample Survey Organization, Department of Statistics, New Delhi, March 1987, (cyclostyled copy).

Government of Maharashtra : *Dr. Babasaheb Ambedkar Writings and Speeches*, Vol. 2, Education Department, Bombay, 1982.

Joshi, N.V. : *Pune Varnana* (Marathi), Sahitya Sahakar Sangha Prakashan, Bombay, First edition 1868 and Second edition, 1971.

Kulkarni, M G. & Hiramani, A.B. : Art. '*Occupational Pattern in Two Marathwada Villages*—a comparative study'; *Marathwada University Journal*, Vol. XIV No. 2, September 1975.

Lapoint, E.C. & Lapoint, D.N. : Art. '*Socio-economic Mobility Among Village Harijans*' in *The Eastern Anthropologist*, Vol. No. 38, No. 2, Jan.-Feb. 1985.

Mehta, Savita *et al* : Art. '*Changing Correspondence Between Caste and Occupation*—a socio-economic analysis' in *The Eastern Anthropologist*, Vol. 37, No. 14, Oct.-Dec. 1984.

Parmar, Y.A. : Art *'Occupational Change Among Mahyavanshisa—Scheduled Caste'* in *The Indian Journal of Social Work*, Vol. No. XXXIX, October 1978.

Patwardhan, Sunanda : *Change Among India's Harijans*; Orient Longman, 1973.

Rahate, J.V. : *Modernization Among Scheduled Castes With Special Reference to Mahars*, Weavers and Sweepers of Nagpur City (Marathi); Ph.D. dissertation (unpublishcd), Marathwada University, Aurangabad, 1985.

Saberwal, S. : Art. *'Receding Pollution : Intercaste Relation in Punjab'* in *Sociological Bulletin*, Vol. 22, 1973.

Santhakumari, R.: *Scheduled Caste and Welfare Measures*; Classical Publishing Company, New Delhi.

Sarkar, Jayanta : *Caste, Occupation and Change*; B.R. Publishing, Delhi, 1984.

Sharma, R.S. : *Shudras in Ancient India*, Motilal Banarsidass, 1958.

Shyamlal : *The Bhangis in Transition*; Inter-India New Delhi, 1984.

Tiwari, Chitra : *Shudras in Manu*; Motilal Banarasidass, 1963.

ELEVEN

Social Development Through New Institutions and Scheduled Castes in The Rural Setting

Dr. Jagdish Kumar Pundir

Most of the connotations of development are preoccupied with the economic, the material and the physical dimensions of human life. These connotations have overlooked the socio-cultural aspects of development. Some sociologists have pleaded for this missing dimension by emphasizing on socio-cultural quality of life as essence of social development. How far change in the quality of life (i.e., social development) has been possible, may be as a consequence of new institutions, in India since independence ? The present paper takes note of such changing aspects which correspond to dimension of social development. It is attempted from the stand point of the Scheduled Castes in rural situations. Whether variation in rural social structures (with regard to dominant caste) also makes a difference ? These are the issues attempted in this paper. The paper is divided into three parts. In the first part the operational connotation of social development, which takes note of socio-cultural quality of life, is arrived at. In the second section the relevant observations in the two types of social structures of four villages are incorporated. The process of social development is examined in the last section i.e. how in the light of new institutions since Independence the social development is taking place in the rural social situations and how the varying social structures respond to this ?

I

Connotation of Social Development

In the works of early social scientists the word development was used to refer to the course of social evolution. In this perspective *growth* was implied in development. The central element of the thinking, that came up in western industrial capitalism, was the idea of economic growth measured in GNP. The concept of development further emphasized in this century when many countries of the third world attained freedom from colonial rule and confronted the problem of reconstruction. Later the word development got redefined as redistribution with growth. Thereafter the concept of development was re-interpreted as an effort to provide for the basic needs of the people, measured in terms of the provisions of necessary goods and services or an increase in the life chances of people. The situation of dependency of poor, underdeveloped nations on developed countries brought in a new conceptualization of development—as *liberation from dependency and exploitation*, measured in terms of enhanced opportunities for masses to obtain their just share in resources. Reviewing the above conceptions S.L. Sharma (1986 : 1—22) made an attempt to formulate socio-cultural dimension of development. He rejects economic or coeconomic dimensions since all these conceptions have resulted into despised category of morality, social indiscipline, anomie, loss of humanity, and man reduced to an in human machine. It is degeneration not development. According to Sharma (1986 : 20) development has to be conceived in holistic terms. Accordingly development may be defined as *improvement in the overall quality of life including the physical, the psychological, the social and cultural.* ......The improvement in the social quality of life means an increase in the strength of family stability, *interpersonal bonds* and social solidarity. The cultural quality of life which has to do with the *moral order of society*...needs to be emphasized....The improvement in cultural quality of life signifies the upsurge of the moral dimension. ......*A concern for others is the essence of social morality*...... for a society to be truely developed a concern for others is a moral imperative. There is need to salvage the concept of development from too much of economics and to put it on the pedestal of sound socio-cultural foundations (Sharma, 1986 : 21).

According to D'Souza (1986 : 103) when the concept of development first came into general acceptance it referred mainly to economic growth. *Even though* the idea of solving some of the pressing social problems such as *inequalities and poverty* was present....The idea was that Growth in some regions and some sections...would gradually trickle down all regions. In other words economic growth was assumed to be an independent variable and various other problems of under development were dependent upon it....Such planning have not transformed societies into desirable patterns....It is therefore now realized that if the ultimate aim of development is the *improvement of the quality of life* of the common man... it cannot be accomplished as an indirect consequence of economic growth...in the ultimate analysis development should stand for the enabling of a person to live *to be* rather than to live *to have*. A developed individual is one who is self-reliant, creative and sociable. The development of such a personality is also contingent upon the building up of an appropriate social structure.

D'Souza has observed that in India traditional caste system militates against the developmental goals of fostering *self reliance, creativity and sociability* among the members of society. Various groups (castes) are mutually exclusive for purposes of intimate relations and sociability.

After having reviewed the review of concept of development we may operationally consider social development as liberation from dependency and exploitation, improvement in the overall quality of life including physical, psychological and socio-cultural, sense of concern for others as social morality, reducing the problems of inequality and poverty, enabling a person to live *to be* rather than live *to have*, by being *self-reliant*, *creative* and *sociable*. And by implication coming out of the exclusiveness of intimate relations based on caste within. Some of the characterstics from the above of the connotation of social development examined here are—breaking the exclusiveness of the caste based intimate relationships, liberation from dependency and exploitation that is achieving of socio-economic self-reliance at individual and group level. How far this type of social development is taking place in rural social situations ? This is examined on the basis of the situation described in the next section of the paper.

II

Two seats of two villages each are taken up here in which the trend of social development are observed. One set is designated as dominant caste rural social structure and other as non-dominant caste rural social structure based the presence or absence of dominant caste in the village setting. Common featurers of the villages are reflected in terms of multi-religious, multi-caste, irrigated land, situated in the agriculturally developed region of western Uttar Pradesh. Common institutional changes introduced are land consolidation, land ceiling, land distribution, introduction of financial, cooperative and other institutions. The universal adult franchise and electioneering has been institutionalized in all the four settings.

The Social Situation : One-Dominant Caste Rural Social Structure

Two villages characterised by the presence of dominant caste are described here. Both are canal watered, large size villages. One is situated in Meerut district. It is a cluster of three in separable villages in terms of village habitation boundaries. The population of this cluster is more than 28000. The Jat caste is the dominant caste of the village-since it is numerically preponderant, owns major part of village land, sufficiently high in ritual status in the caste hierarchy, modern education and occupation are taken by large number, and has a say in the political affairs of the region. The other caste numerically significant is Chamar. They are occupationally divided into three groups—raw leather workers, tanned leather workers and shoe makers, and agricultural and allied labourers. A few have got land allotted to them under the new land reforms policies. Earlier this caste depended directly for labour work upon the higher land owning castes, the Jats. The group of permanent agricultural labourers has shifted to casual and contractual labour and also work on their own land, use their buffalo carts and milch buffaloes for earning their livelihood. The institutions of electioneering have influenced their contact with higher castes, but a little in this situation. Under the planned development efforts they are recipients of land pieces, loans for buffalo-carts and milk buffaloes from the banks. The leather workers have also received loans for their work. No permanent labourer is attached to a high caste farmer now as it was the case in 1950's when hundreds of them were working as 'hali' and 'naukars' to the high caste, the Jats. In dinning on the occasion of marriages etc. Chamar stand apart from the high caste.

In the background of these institutional measures now the Chamar caste stands separate, still at a distance in day to day and ritual occasions from the dominant caste. On the first occasion of getting loans from the commercial banks under the lead bank scheme a few had taken loans for their self employment purposes—sepecially for buffalo carts, milk buffalo and leather work. In this process they were discouraged by dominant caste persons and no (except one) guarantees for them were provided by any high caste person* at the very first phase of financing by commercial bank (Pundir, 1978, 1988).

Other dominant caste rural social structure is a case of a Rajput village in district Saharanpur. Again it is a large size village of approximately 12000 population. Rajput consititute more than 50% of the population. Rajput is by all characterstics a dominant caste of the village. It is the village,** where at first the Community Development Project was introduced in the first five year plan in 1952. The new institutional arrangements have introduced a new urban culture. One part of the village stands separate, where a college, bank office, cooperative society office, hospital (PHC) etc. are situated. In between the village and this complex a market, a bus stand have come up. Several Scheduled Caste persons have undertaken new ventures like a repair shop of rubber the carts, shoe, cycle etc. In this village the distance with the high caste in dinning has been reduced a little. The Chamars are invited to sit on chairs, stools; food and tea in the utencils and cups by Rajputs on various occasions and also in routine matters whenever it is needed. The Chamars are invited to take even drinks during the electioneering of Panchayat elections. During the marriages they are offered food alongwith other caste persons sitting on

* This has been dealt in dealt in detail in J.K. Pundir, 1988, "Lead Banks and Traditional Money-landing Institutions in The Rural Setting," Ph.D. Thesis, Meerut University.

** Described as a Rajput Village in *India's Changing Villages* by S.C. Dube (1958).

The Institutions in this rural setting and their consequences are given in J.K. Pundir "Urban Institutions in Rural Setting" *Samajiki* Vol. 3 (New Series), No. 2, 1982, pp. 38-46,

the earth in a line. In occupational and economic dependency many of them work as 'naukars' but not 'halis' as was the case earlier. Daily wage labour and contractual labour has become prevalent practice in the agricultural operations. Another larger number of Chamar are working in allied agricultural activities. Thus some changes, though the difference is in degrees from the Jat village are observed. Here also the institution of 'hali' stands abolished. The Scheduled Castes have taken loans in a few number while a bank's branch exists in the village itself.

The Social Situation: Two Non-Dominant Caste Rural Social Structure

Observations were carried out in other two villages. The common factor in both the villages is that no caste in these villages can be characterized as a dominant caste. Both the villages are irrigated in large part by pump sets and tubewells and not by canal water which is the case with the earlier two.

The first village* is situated in Meerut district on the border of the U.P. State touching on the otherside across Yamuna river the Haryana State. This village is composed of 37 different Hindu (18) and Muslim (17) castes and Jain (2) social groups. With regard to relations of Chamar and the High Hindu Caste Tyagi, observations show that the Chamars are invited in the marriages. The Chamars sit with the Tyagi on the cots. In the marriages Chamar are served food together with the Tyagi sitting on the same chairs and tables like other guests. Even at one instance they were served food alongwith the 'Barat' on the tables. The Tyagi have an interdependent relation of Nyota'**

* The details of new Institutions since independence are given in J.K. Pundir "Village Life—Towards Pluralism" in I.N. Tiwary et. al. (eds). *Challenges and Alternatives*, 1980, Pub. by U.P. Political Science Association.

** The details are given in J.K. Pundir Ibid., 1988.

with the Chamars. The High Caste Tyagi and others supported the Scheduled Castes, Chamars and Valmikis, in taking loans from the bank. They extended crucial support in giving guarantees for the Chamars and Valmiki (for more than 2/3) to the bank at the first phase of financing in 1976 (Pundir, 1978, 1988).

The Scheduled Castes are categorized mainly into three occupational groups – the leather workers, the wage labourers, and working on their own either on land or shop and mixed. The permanent agricultural labour (hali) has been replaced in the village by daily wage and contractual labour in agricultural operations. The Chamars and Valmiki are comparatively free. The electioneering has further divided the higher castes and brought the Chamars closer than earlier. In this situation a vertical division and association of castes is visible. The Chamars are also divided in extending the support to the high castes. The Chamars themselves have further some closer by becoming Up-Pradhans more than twice in the village panchayat. Most of the Chamars and Valmiki stand more self sufficient and confident in their occupations. A few have shifted to milk buffaloes, shopkeeping, refined leather work, service and vegetable growing on the newly acquired land under the new institutional arrangements. Such land is available in the basin of the river where other people also grow vegetables. The economic dependency upon higher castes has gradually weakened. The daily wage labourers are working for fixed hours, asking higher wages during peak season and working in contractual groups.

The last situation is of a village in Hardwar district of western U.P. The village is composed of twenty Hindu castes and five Muslim caste like endogamous groups. No caste is there which is numerically significant, can be designated as dominant caste. The two ritually high castes the Jats and the Chauhan are big land owner-cultivator castes and are mutually competing groups. The two castes have also been competing for power position in the village as well. But the Jats have never succeeded. Their competition has led to lower caste persons becoming village Pradhans.

The intercaste relations with the lowest castes particularly with the Chamars stand changed. Most of the land owners in 1950's had at least one 'hali' (permanent agricultural labourer) from among the Chamars. The number of 'halis' was more than 80 in the 1950's. Now not even a single 'hali' is there in the village. The ex-'halis' who used to cultivate for the farmers of high castes now cultivate their newly gained, own land under new institutional arrangements by their own bullocks. Also a few are earning by having buflalo carts. Another few are working as semiskilled mechanics, shopkeepers, venders, in and outside the village. Casually during the harvest and peak agricultural season they work as contractual labour. During the elections at village level the Chamar are invited for drinks, dinning, sit together with high castes. On the occasion of marriages they are invited by high castes—Jat, Chauhan, Rajput and others. The Chamars are served food in the same pangat (line of guests and invitee villagers) by higher castes. Chauhans have been more liberal than Jats in bridging the gap between them. Jat are less open on this score of interdinning.

In taking loans from the financial institutions the Scheduled Castes have been supported by high castes particularly by those who were influential in the election fray. The village surplus lands have been granted to a large number of Chamars. A few Jat and a Chauhan fought litigation on this issue for years. The agricultural labourers and their fathers, used to work as permanent agricultural labourers (hali) for some higher castes, are now completely free from that. Only casual labour, more so contractual labour, is available now. The higher caste land owners are forced to cultivate their own land more or less by themselves. A few persons from other lower castes like Gadaria (shephered), Banjara have started working as wage labourers and contractual labourers. Only a couple of Chamars are working as 'naukars' for high caste land owners, none as a 'hali'.

III

After describing briefly the social situations in the two types of villages which are designated as dominant caste rural social structures and the other non-dominant caste social structures we can examine the issues raised in the beginning of the paper. Since the Independence achieved in 1947, several institutional measurers have been introduced in the rural settings. Those have come to be known as planned efforts of development. Initially the emphasis was to develop the totality of economic production and other changes will follow. Later on it was modified into redistribution of resources also. In the first category land consolidation may be considered which was intended at increasing production. The others, related to land ownership in the villages, are land ceiling and redistribution of village surplus land to the landless; particularly the Scheduled Castes. New schemes of financing for self employment of the landless have come into being. Health, legal and other measurers what soever, are going on. Thus upto a dozen of agencies' functionaries are observed in the rural, setting. Some of these have had impact on the social life.

On the growth of new institutional measures a few changes have occured. Some of those are indicators of social development. All through the illustrations of village situation it is observed that social distance between higher castes and lower castes, particularly with the ex untouchable Chamar has reduced. The exclusiveness of caste has broken upto some extent as the vertical division and association is visible. Eating, drinking, sitting, working of higher castes and untouchables together prove this. The economic dependence of lowest castes upon higher castes has reduced considerably. This to some extent reduced the exploitation of lower castes by the higher castes.

In this sense the ex-untouchables are moving towards selfsufficiency in occupational matters by way of working on their own land and other occupations and comparatively free from permanent labour involving some exploitation, free labour, credit etc. Further the difference of degrees is observed between the dominant caste social structure and non-dominant caste social structure. Presence of dominant caste lead to less decreasing of social distance and mixing up. Non-dominant caste social structure proves more favourable in lessening the social distance. Occupational self reliance and autonomy is common consequence of the growth of new institutional measures in both types of social structural situations. Commonality of bringing together the traditionally hitherto existing distanced castes is reflected in many individuals from among the lower castes (particularly Scheduled Caste-Chamar) who are coming closer. At group level as a whole this needs further final confirmations.

Lastly, we can put the findings into propositional form. Greater the introduction of new institutional measures leads to lessening the social distance between castes i.e. if more new institutions grow then the social distance between higher and lower castes decreases, sociability increases. Secondly, if new institutions grow then dependency and exploitation of lower castes decreases. The variation in the type of social structure responds to variation in bridging the social distance and sociability but less it is related in economic sphere i.e., comparatively lesser and occupational dependency and freedom from exploitation.

References

D'Souza, Victor S. 1986 : "Social Structural Constraints on Development" in S.L. Sharma (ed). *Development-Socio-Cultural Dimensions.* Jaipur, Rawat-Publications, pp. 103-111.

Pundir, J.K. 1980 : "Indian Rural Life-Pluralist View" in I.N. Tiwary et. al. (eds.) *Challenges and Alternatives,* U.P. Political Science Asaociation, pp. 24-32, (Hindi).

1982 : "Urban Institutions in Rural Setting," Samajiki (New Series) Vol. 3, No. 2, pp. 38-46.

1988 : "Lead Banks and Traditional Maney-lending Institutions in The Rural Setting," unpublished Ph.D. Thesis, Meerut University.

Sharma, S.L. 1986 : "Changing Conceptions of Development—An Analytical Search for Missing Dimension" in S.L. Sharma (ed.) *Development : Socio-Cultural Dimensions,* Jaipur, Rawat Publications, pp, 1-22.

TWELVE

Scheduled Castes in Transition

Dr. P.N. Khare

According to traditional Hindu Social Organization of India, Hindu society is divided in five stratas i.e. Brahmins, Kshtriyas, Vaishyas, Shudras and the Antyajas. According to sociologists this fifth fold i.e. the Panchamas are called by various names, viz.—Backward Hindus, Untouchables, Awarnas, etc. Gandhiji called them 'Harijans', the most beloved to God. In British officialese, some time in late 19th century the term "depressed classes" was used for the untouchables. A few social Anthropologists used it for tribes also. After 1932 the term" Scheduled Castes" came into practice to identify the Pancham Varna of Indian Society. After the attainment of India's Independence, the Government of India has continued to accord an independent status to this category of Indian population, for constitutional protection and developmental allocations.

In the present paper an attempt has been made to understand and underscore the nature of change that is taking place among the Scheduled Castes on the basis of research studies—conducted by the Social Scientists.

Traditionally the members of these castes suffered lots of disabilities in regard to food, water, clothing, wearing of ornaments etc. and they had to maintain social distance with the other four folds of Hindu Society which are above them on social ladder. In the rural and urban areas the untouchables had to eat 'Jhuttan'. They could not use the same well or tank which other upper caste members of the society were using. Bathing Ghats were different, they had to use customary black clothes. They were prohibited to use silver ornaments, they could not ride the horse, could not go out in the day time, they had to shout for their existance. Thus Scheduled Castes were born in pollution, and they lived and died in pollution. Similarly they were denied to enter into the temples and were denied admission to schools. They had to perform forced labour i.e. Begar. The so-called masters were used to punish them on this or that pretext. They were beaten every day, even the bodies were burned and women raped.

The District Gazetters, Census reports, Ethnographers, Anthropologists, and Sociologists like Ghurye, Shriniwas, Bailey, Basu, S K., Andre Beteille, Bhatt G.S., Atre, Shinde, Mate and Sunanda Patwardhan have described the disabilities suffered by the then untouchables. In Indian villages they were denied the services of Brahmins, Barber, Tailor, Waterman etc.

Dr. B.R. Ambedkar in his famous book "The Untouchables" wrote that "the notion of defilement, of pollution and contamination by touch is at the basis of untouchability. Defilement as such is not peculiar to Indian Society."

Notion of defilement prevalent among the Hindus is not different from that which obtained in primitive societies, but there is another form of untouchability observed by the Hindus......it is the hereditary untouchability of certain communities." He has further added that" they are born impure, they are impure while they live. They have the death of the impure and they give birth to children who are born with the stigma of untouchability affixed to them.

In the countryside they did not own any agricultural land. In fact traditionally they are prohibited to do so. They earned very meagre incomes and were indebted generation to generation. Thus they were leading a very miserable life.

Social reform movement as one of the sources of change was initiated by Mahatma Gandhi at the national level and by Mahatma Jyotiba Phule of Maharashtra at the Regional level. They were opposed by many traditional Hindu Brahmins and other elites of then India, some of the social reform movements among Scheduled Castes involved the adoption of the style of life and values of the upper castes. They had notion that if they adopt the values and norms of the upper castes their status will improve. The motivation for change was status mobility. They had accepted the food habits (left Group habits) started Idol worship, taken various Gods and upper caste names. In the social organization field they had left their original traditional practice of widow remarriage. Sunanda Patwardhan in her research work found that—"Inferior status accorded to the widow who remarries in a Sanskritic Braminical value, widow remarriage is considered an inferior form of marriage by the Harijans including neo-Buddhists. She has also noticed religion and the relevance of Sanskritization in her urban sample of the Harijans studied.

Due to social reform movements and adoption of the style of life and values of the upper castes, some cases of confrontation occured, because the upper castes like Brahmins and Thakurs did not tolerate that these people should compete with them. In relation to ritual status, the untouchables of Indian villages started performing Agni Pooja and desired to wear Sacred-thread i.e. 'Yatnopavit'.

In one village of Porsa Block of Morena district in M.P., dominant Thakurs have burnt Harijans back and front shoulder below area of boby, where sacred-thread rests, with the help of a Iron-rod saying "this is a permanent Yagnopavit for you" to those who desired to wear sacred-thread.

One of the important variant of social reform movements was conversion to other religious faith. Conversion leads to socio-economic improvements of the converts. Conversion took place to Buddhism, Christianity, Islam and Sikhism. Research studies showed that even after the conversion their identification as Scheduled Castse continued in rural India.

Similarly they are looked upon as a lower group within the group of reference. Thus social differentiation continued to persist, each category maintaining characteristics of a caste. In the States of U.P. and M.P. converted Scheduled Caste members are still identified by their original caste-names. Their antecedent low ritual status and poor economic resources, coupled with occupational identification, prevented them from establishing equal relationships with higher caste members. But it can not be denied that many Scheduled Castes improved their material conditions and emancipated themselves from traditional ritual degradation, although to a limited extent, through conversions.

Indian Constitution provides for a number of protective measures for the welfare of the Scheduled Castes, chief measures include :—

(a) Representation in the Parliament and State Legislatures (of late the period of such reservations increased upto 2000 A.D.)

(b) Representations in the Central Services.

(c) Representations in the State Services.

(d) Special provisions for Social Educational and Economic advancement.

(e) Banning of traffic human beings and forced labour.

In addition to this to raise the Social and Economic status of the untouchables in 1955 "The Untouchability Offences Act" was passed. The provision has been made to appoint a special officer to investigate all matters relating to safeguards provided for the Scheduled Castes.

Introduction of Panchayat Raj provided Scheduled Castes to represent themselves in Panchayats and local bodies. But still they are not nominated in high power committees and thus they are kept away from decision making process.

Due to serious disabilities faced by Scheduled Castes in India, they remained illiterate and ignorant. During British regime, the erst-while States of Bombay and Baroda, Madras, Travancore and in M.B. State—Holkar State have thrown open all the streets, temples, schools, wells, etc. to the untouchables.

Till Independence and even after Independence Scheduled Caste students were not allowed to mix with others children of upper castes in schools. Even if they were admitted to schools, they were asked to sit in a separate line, which has been observed by the author in many Indian villages. They are discouraged by the teachers and sometimes they have been asked to go away and not to come again.

In a Gandhi Smarak Nidhi sponsored survey the Harijan Sevak Sangh claimed that the dragon of untouchability has been overpowered. The Sangh reported that "untouchability is vanishing from many areas."

The caste Hindus had began to rent out their houses to the untouchables and that Inter-caste common feasts were organized on many occasions in Kerala and the U.P. The Sangh also reported the peaceful cradication of such social disabilities as Harijan entry into the temples. Their using public wells, restaurants, and services of Barbers and Washernmen, denied to them earlier.

The reports also claim that the psychological foundations of untouchability have been undermined and a change of heart among caste Hindus seems to have taken place.

The Sangh reported undertaking a number of amneliorative welfare programmes among the untouchables including opening of Balvadis and Creches.

Sangh have also undertaken programme preventive drinking and gambling among Harijans. Obtaining admission of Harijans to educational institutions; educating Harijan women in the art of decent and healthy family life.

In author's research study (1964) observations have been made that many Harijan women earners have started living neatly and cleanly. Their kitchens were well arranged, utensils were very clean; when they go out for work or for shopping they wear clean saries. Thus they have developed the concept of living neatly and pleasantly.

Of late Harijan Sevak Sangh have introduced Non-conventional crafts and opened new areas of employment, such as truck/bus driving, carpentry, vegetable, fruit vendors, welding, spinning etc. Many Harijans are working in Textile Mills of M.P. They also claimed to have introduced special Bhangi Mukti and Bhangi Kasht Mukti Programmes involving abolishing scavangers as a class and abolition of unclean methods of cleaning dry latrines.

The changing pattern of status can not be same all over India as a few studies indicated that in many middle class and lower middle class households social distance with the untouchables is still maintained. Separate utensils or pots are kept for them for serving them tea or meals etc. Although they are treated in a normal manner, the pollution is in the minds of men, and it is very difficult to separate pollution from human out look.

Takulia wrote that "All over Rural Panjab, where there are no hand-pumps, villages still have separate drinking wells for them, separate Gurudwaras for the Sikhs of Scheduled Caste origin are quite common.

He further wrote "that a physical contact causes ritual pollution is a fact of life for many "Mazhabi Sikhs". Accepting water from some of the lower castes is rather a more prevalent phenomenon among sects of the Sikhs. For example among Nihangs, untouchability is practised to fetch wood for the langer, (Community Meals) but not allowed to cook or serve the food.

Author has observed at one marriage occasion in M.P., the hosts have invited a few Harijan factory workers for marriage feast in Indore. One state minister was also invited. Although there was a separate line i.e. Pangat for the untouchables to sit for dinner, the then minister stood up and went without taking meals. While the practice of discrimination no longer exists, it does not mean that untouchability is dying out rapidly. It will take time to clear the minds of men. In post-independent period until recently anti-Scheduled Castes rioting reported. At many places untouchables were beaten, women raped by gangs of people. In Belchi the Harijans were lined up for being shot and tossed into an already prepared funeral pyre. At many places they were burnt alive in their own houses.

In Bihar, U.P., M.P., Tamil Nadu and Karnataka incidences of violence under IPC recorded in thousands during 70s and 80s.

In regard to maltreatment by the members of the upper castes to the untouchables, it is imperative that the members of the upper castes to whom Harijans are related due to occupation or any other work, be adviced to change their behaviour pattern, have humanitarian view point, and keep healthy relationship with them. In this process office bearers of Harijan Sevak Sangh, Indore were very active. Periodically members and social workers are visiting upper caste for changing their hearts.

It can be concluded that constitutional safeguards, state action, reservations and even conversions have not much affected the status of Scheduled Caste in India. They are to be educated and schemes be framed for the occupational rehabilitation of the Harijans particularly in rural areas. Gandhi's prescription to the untouchables was education, self improvement and patient self-suffering for a change of heart among the caste Hindu.

It this is processed at the national and Regional level and village level untouchability will die out slowly.

References

1. Ambedkar, B.R, *Who were the Shudras*, 1946.

   The Untouchables, who were and why they become untouchables, 1948 Amrit Book Co., Delhi.

2. Bailey, F.G. *Caste and the Economic Frontier*, 1957.

3. Bhatt, G.S. *Trends aud Measurements of Social Mobility among the Chamars of Dehradun*,' 1961, Eastern Anthropologists, Vol. XIV, No. 3, pp. 229-241.

4. Khare, P.N. *A Study of Women Earners in Indore*, 1964, (Ph.D. dissertation) unpublished.

   Slum dwellers of Labherpura Research Paper 1961, (Mimeographed).

5. Mayer, A.C. *Caste and Kinship in Central India, A village and its Region*. 1960, University of of California Press, Berkeley & Los Angelas.

6. Patwardhan, Sunanda *Change among India's Harijans-Maharashtra A Case Study*, 1973, Orient Longmans Ltd.

7. P.S. Jannu *Untouchability Among Shikhs*, a paper presented at a seminar held in 1983 at

Punjab University, Chandigarh organized by the Department of Sociology.

8. Takulia, H.S. '*Removal of Untouchability A Gandhian Perspective*' *in Social Development Processes & Consequences*, 1989, Edited by P.N. Pimpley & Others.

9. *Indian Express*, Chandigarh, 5.2.84, p. 5.

10. *Tribune*, Chandigarh, 12.10.86, p. 5.

THIRTEEN

Differential Consequences of Rural Development of Weaker Sections

A Case Study of A Mircrosetting in Meerut

Dr. Jagdish Kumar Pundir

Rural development has been considered in several meanings. One is that rural development means development of new institutions for the betterment of the rural people. In India since Independence several institutional arrangements have come to operate from outside, mainly under State policy, on the village scene. The rural social structure provides the field for operation of all these institutions. In what way the social structure interacts with such institutions ? Whether the social structure digests the gains even when the gains are meant for a particular section ? *When it is meant for weaker sections* (*i.e. Scheduled Castes*) *whether really weaker are benefitted* ? And in what way it interacts with the traditional institutions existing for the same purposes ? In brief what are the differential consequences of an institution reaching the village under the cover rural development ?

The above questions are attempted in this paper in relation to the commercial bank reaching the *rural weaker sections* (*i.e. Scheduled Castes*) *for financing their self employment schemes.* The complexity of the process, of meeting the urban based, formal, commercial organization (Commercial Bank) which for the first time reached the neglected, economically poor and socially lowest section of the community, which was never touched before, is explored. The concept of differential functionalism (Merton : 1968) is used as an analytical tool here universe of the study is a village community in Western Uttar where the District Lead Bank (Syndicate Bank) financed the Pradesh *weaker sections for the first time, the Harijans of the village.* Scheduled Castes are operationally termed as Weaker Sections throughout this paper. Later on other banks also joined hands for such people for other purpose namely the biogas instalations.

The paper is divided into four sections. The first section takes note of the village social structure. In the second section a brief of traditional and other money lending institutions is given. The process of the new banking institution alongwith a profile of the initial recipients and the intermediaries are given in third section. In the fourth section the analysis is attempted to arrive at the answers to the questions raised.

I. The Village Social Structure

The village, 'Kotana,' is situated on the eastern bank of river Yamuna, bordering Haryana State, in district Meerut of western Uttar Pradesh. It is sixty kilometers north of the national capital Delhi and at the same distance towards west from the district head-quarter Meerut. The village is approached through a metalled link road from a near by town Baraut (most important town of the famous constituency of ex-Prime Minister Ch. Charan Singh). The village is to be known as an ancient inhabited village of the region since the time of Mahabharata. In ninteenth century before the development of railways and

Yamuna canals it was a commerical centre of agricultural produce and known as a town. Later on the river transport abondoned, it ruined consequently important business houses left for Delhi and the nearby growing town. It is a village now and there is a pragana in its name.

It is a multireligious, multicaste village consisting of Hindus, Muslims and Jains (Swetambri and Digambar). Before Jamidari Abolition in Uttar Pradesh Jains, a Pathan an another Muslims Kazi families were the landlords. Tyagis living in the village have been big landowners having their land in the name of an adjacent uninhabited village till recently. According to voters list analysis there are 21 castes of Hindus, two groups of Jains and 16 castes or caste like groups of Muslims exist in the village, Brahmin, Tyagi, Rave, Jat among Hindus, Jains (both groups), Pathan, Rohella Pathan among the Muslims constitute the upper leader in the traditional social hierarchy. Whereas Julaha, Khatik, Chamar, Valmiki, Sikligar among Hindus and Sakkai, Kasai (who are actual butchers), Julaha, Faquir (Jogi) constitute the lowest leader in the traditional social hierarchy in the village.

Since the emergence of village Panchayat the Pradhans have always been drawn from the upper social strata. At the first time in 1949 a Brahmin occupied the post who handed over within a year the office to a Tyagi, then a Jain succeeded him from 1955 to 1962. Soon after Jain becoming Block Pramukh a Rohella Pathan turned him down in 1963 for next one decade. Again in 1972 the same Jain got the chair through election. In the next election in 1982 the same Rohella Pathan elected to the office and continuing. The village, thus, could also participate in the block level politics as the first Tyagi Pradhan become up-Block Pramukh and the Jain Pradhan becoming Block Pramukh in 1963 of Baraut Block. Two persons from among the Scheduled Castes came on the scene as up Pradhans, earlier an old one and in eighties a middle aged Chamar. The Chamars have also been found actively participating as elected Panchayat members from among the younger generation. They could come in some conflicts with the high castes Hindus and Muslims in disputes arising out of their harassment, land distribution and theft and killing cases (Pundir, 1980 : 64-68).

Beyond the village a few persons like the late Jain Pradhan's sons have their business in the nearby town and at distant places like Kanpur. The one from nearby town comes to the village daily, others also come frequently. A few others go for small business and services in the nearby villages, towns, Meerut, Delhi and other cities. A bus service from the village (Started in late 1970's) promoted frequent links. Kinship and such links extend to the bordering State Haryana too. Out of the 8 medical practitioners 7 hail from outside, ranging an area upto 20 or more kilometers. Some thirty odd shops of various kinds also provide day to day outside links of the village. A weekly market has also been started a few years back attracting the petty shop-keepers and customers from the nearby villages and towns. Thus the village gets various connections with the nearby villages, towns and cities even beyond the region.

The chief occupation of higher social groups is mainly agriculture except the Jains who are partially land holders and mainly traders. The middle and low castes depend on agriculture—if they are owner cultivators of small land others on agriculture and other wage labour. In the river basin the vegetable growing cuts across the caste or religion boundries. Highest aste as well lowest caste people get engaged in the vegetable and melon growing in the river basin. To the labour force it provides good opportunities. Exceptionally a few Brahmins have small land holdings and a few others among them work as labourers. None of the Brahmin does priestly work. For ceremonies the Brahmins are called from the nearby villages.

Among the Scheduled Castes—a majority of 125 Chamar families have shoe making as an important occupation, partly supplemented by agriculture on newly gained land pieces, agriculture labour and milk cattles. The Valmiki in addition to their traditional occupation scavanging, supplement their earnings by piggery and daily wage labour. The Sikligars depend on their traditional occupation of cheap cost locks making.

II The Money Lending : Traditional and New Arrangements

For essential, ceremonial and social occasions the money lending happened to be professionalized. To satisfy credit need there have been professional money lenders, agriculturists, Jagirdars, traders (Chauhan : 1967, Srinivas : 1976 etc.) In this particular situation the Jains, are recognized professional money lenders. Particularly the late Jain Pradhan's family was the chief money-lender from generations. There are agriculturists like the Pradhan family and a Tyagi family who are recognized money-lenders but the two with a difference. The other pattern is taking buffalo or cattle or bullock on loan from the animal traders who are a Kasai group in this village. On several occasions money used to be borrowed from traders, money lenders of the nearby town.

The use of the river basin for vegetable growing resulted in more income for people on the one hand and needed more investment on the other hand in the beginning. This gave rise to another connections for money lending from the vegetable business men in the nearby towns of the neighbouring State Haryana and also from Delhi. More or less the lowest strata in general and Scheduled Castes in particular remained untouched because they could not enter this business cultivation at a commercial scale rather their opportunities of wage labour increased.

In 1962 the land consolidation was done in the village. This gave rise to the beginning of a new era of the new means of irrigation owned by the individual agriculturists. Though Taqavi loans for digging well were used to be provided earlier also Through Community Development Programme yet this era initiated more and more pumpset-wells. This needed large amounts of money....The Land Development Bank, Co-operative Bank, the Taqavi loans were taken. In addition the Commercial Banks had also appeared on the scene. During the sixtees a tractor loan was also taken. The Commerical Banks thus entered the agriculture...providing loans for pump-sets, seeds, fertilizers and technological implements. But the weaker sections, Scheduled Castes mostly landless were still untouched from such facilities for improving their earnings. They were used to get loans for petty essential social or ceremonial needs, house making or any other need from the private sources i.e. the professional money lenders available in the village and in nearby villages and town. Under the State Policy the Commercial Bank (Lead Bank of the District) entered the village specifically for financing the weaker sections in 1976. The new facility in the rural area has to be seen in terms of the delineation of the recipients into various categories—this time the weaker sections.

III The New Credit Institution and The Process of Loaning

A Commerical Bank (The Lead Bank of Meerut District) has its branch office at Baraut town. The branch selected seven villages in the Baraut block with the consultation of the B.D.O. Kotana is one of them. The loans were given, for the first time in 1976, for productive purposes like dairying, Piggery Fertilizers and other self employment purposes. The process of banking in a new setting derives its initiative from the Government's new policies for the economic development of weaker sections of society. The Government directed the Commerical Banks to provide loans to these sections. The banks ordered their branch offices to do so. In this case in the initial stage of bank invited the persons with the help of the field officer and also got contacted the people with the consent of the B.D.O. On the other hand the people also received information through the means of communication—e.g. mass-media, as well as rural-urban linkages through leading group of persons of the village.

The whole process of getting and utilizing loan involves a number of formalities. How did they get translated into action at village level may now be visualized—

1. The information to the villagers (weaker section) through the elitist group of the village from among the high castes and Scheduled Castes.
2. The Field Officer of the Bank visited the village in this connection to tell about the aims and procedures of getting loan in the last week of June, 1976.
3. Putting the demands of the people and filling of application forms was done in the last days of June, 1976.
4. Savings accounts were opened by the persons Willing to get loans.
5. Clearance certificates from the other formal agencies existing in the area (Co-operative Bank, Tehsil etc.), were obtained and submitted to the bank office. In this the B.D.O. also helped in scrutiny.
6. Sanctioning of loan by the bank authorities.
7. The cheques were given to the recipients on Ist July, 1976 for their manifest purposes e.g. cattle, piggery, rickshaw.
8. The cheques were encashed.
9. Two weeks time was given to use the money for prescribed purposes.
10. The receipts of purchase were submitted within the month of July, 1976.
11. Verification on the spot by the Field Officer of the bank along with the B.D.O. in last week of July, 1976

for checking whether the money had been used for purchasing the things stipulated for.

12. The animals purchased were marked and numbered in the presence of the Field Officer by the veterinary doctor of the Veterinary Hospital of the Block.

The completion of the process had some effect as it happened for the first time in the village. The purpose of loans and the recipients from various social group are given in table 1.

The amount given were for rickshaw Rs. 1000, Biogas plant Rs. 3300 each, Cattles Rs. 2000 each, Fertilizer Rs. 1500 each and piggery Rs. 1000 each. Thus Rs. 1,03,900 were provided.

The loans for biogas plants, were advance before June, 1976, for fertilizer in July and November 1976 and as is clear have gone to the higher groups whereas the loan for cattles has gone largely to the Harijans.

The economic categories from which the recipients are drawn can however be assessed from their size of holdings given in table 2.

Some observations are in order. All the large size holders are drawn from among the higher categories of Hindu and Muslim. The distribution among the landless Harijans is almost equal to that of the land holders. If a line is drawn at 15 bigha, two elites among the Scheduled Castes appear on the scene.

Every recipient according to bank rules, should have to arrange two guarantors. In case of Harijans the guarantors have been drawn from S.C.S. and higher caste groups. Table 3 shows the position of guarantors drawn from among different social groups.

TABLE 1

Loan Recipients and their Social Groups

Social Group/Purpose	*Rickshaw*	*Biogas*	*Cattles*	*Fertilizer*	*Piggery*	*Total*
Harijans (Chamar & Valmiki)	–	–	38	–	3	41
Lower Muslims	1	–	3	–	–	4
Lower Hindu	–	–	1	–	–	1
Other Farmers (Hindu & Muslim)	–	3	–	4	–	7
Total	1	3	42	4	3	53

TABLE 2

Size of Holdings of the Recipients of Loan

Land Holding/Social Group	*Harijan*	*Lower Muslim*	*Lower Hindu*	*Higher Hindu & Muslim*	*Total*
Nil	21	1	—	—	22
1—$7\frac{1}{2}$—Bigha	6	—	1	—	7
8 to 15 Bigha	12	—	—	—	12
16 to 30 Bigha	2	3	—	—	5
More than 30 Bigha	—	—	—	7	7
Total	41	4	1	7	53

TABLE 3

Guarantors of the Recipients Among Different Social Groups (Two in each Case)

S. No.	*Recipients/ Guarantors*	*Brahmin*	*Tyagi*	*Jain*	*Pathan*	*Sekh*	*Harijan*	*Other*	*Total*
1.	Harijan (41)	4	22	16	6	3	30	1	82
2.	Lower Hindu (1)	—	—	1	—	—	1	—	2
3.	Lower Muslim	—	2	2	1	—	1	2	8
4.	Others Farmers (7)	—	8	—	1	1	—	4	14
	Total (58)	4	32	19	8	4	32	7	106

The guarantors are drawn from among all sections of the village community. They not merely indicate that they stand as surities but also the need for well placed persons on the part of the recipients in utilizing a measurement for their benefit. Over two thirds of the loans for the weaker sections bear testimony of some one from among the higher groups. Social relations with them and a mutuality of obligations to them over a long period have got to be negotiated if this system were to continue.

Only 32 out of 106 guarantees have been made by Harijans where 9 of them have done in more than one cases each. Only four among them have not got the loans. On the other hand among the non-Harijan guarantors only 4 have made use of the facility.

In processing the information some five-six persons came into light frequently—The village School Head Master (a Tyagi) guaranteed in 14 cases; a Jain (the than Pradhan) and his son guaranteed in 10 cases each. The Pradhan at present who was at that time ex-Pradhan, a Rohella Pathan, in 9 cases, a Brahmin and another Tyagi in 4 cases each, a Chamar in 4 cases and another one in 3 cases. These persons have been helpful to the recipients in the process of taking and utilizing loan.

There are some 150 house holds of Harijans (Chamar, Valmiki, and Sikligar) in the village out of whom 41 persons could make use of the new facility. In a few house holds more than one persons are recipients. Thus the beneficiary families remained only 29. In addition to remaining 120 Harijan house holds there are other economically and socially weaker sections like the Jhinwar, Khatik, Teli, Kasai, Mallah, Sikligar etc., who are left untouched from the facility.

Now a look at the second stage of loaning in which the Agricultural Development Branch of the State Bank of India, financed for the biogas plants to the weaker sections in the village in the next year i.e. 1977. Eighteen biogas plants were financed. Out of 18, 17 were among the Harijans of village Kotana. The process of formalities and completion of the steps as were indicated in first case were done mostly by the leading Harijans themselves. One Tyagi, a landless, and an active problem solving person also got it under the same apprehension as for the Scheduled Castes. The B.D.O. who was also a Scheduled Caste was the forwarding or in a sense big intermediary acted promptly in the financing of the projects. The B.D.O., the Bank and the manufacturer/supplier of the equipment were situated in the same town. The manufacturer was the eldest son of the late Jain Pradhan of Kotana having his biogas plant manufacturing and supplying business in the town. In this case the information passed on by the B.D.O. being a S/C to the S.C. people, a Tyagi (key person) and the leading Harijans in the village. The B.D.O. made them understand that there was upto 75% subsidy from the various agencies on biogas for the weaker sections. On the other hand the loans of the first timc (financed by the Lead Bank) were also pending.

The guarantors (majority of higher castes) of the earlier cases were also being issued notices for non-payment of instalements. So they were also interested that they should be relieved from the surities if the loans could be repayed. The office of State Bank as a formality needed no objection certificate from the earlier bank. Thus when educated about the benefits of subsidy, saving out of it, and repayment of the earlier bank loan, B.D.O's on target of planting biogas to show his block at the top in the region, combined together motivated the Harijans to go for biogas loans.

The payment of the earlier loans was needed to have clearance for next loan. Thus there was need to flow money for the purpose. The B.D.O. and his officials, the key person Tyagi, the manufacturer of the bio-plants (eldest son of the Jain

Pradhan), leading Harijans came together joining underhand dealings thus 17 biogas were financed for Harijans. The money in terms of commissions and profits flown. The village level worker on behalf of the B.D.O. to manage the affairs. In addition the target completion of officials of Agricultural Development Branch of the State Bank and motivation by higher caste people of the village who were guarantors in the earlier case facilitated the process. All the guarantees were provided by the recipients themselves under the group guarantee scheme. They did not need the higher caste people this time, the earlier guarantors were also reluctant this time.

Thus of the 17 persons who opted biogas plants' loans mostly (12) were earlier recipients too. Only two plants actually started working in one year, of official installation. Thereafter non of the bio-gas plants worked. Even most of the other 16 were never completed. This was a case of transfer of technology exclusively meant for rural area which involved many steps where the formal financing agency, the intermediary agency for rural development in the Block office, the other intermediaries the manufacturer/supplier and the higher caste people worked at different levels with different interests in negotiating the process of financing the biogas plants.

Different agencies had different meanings of the same process and so different aims and objectives as the B.D.O. number of biogas plants installed in his block, for the bank completion of target of financing weaker sections upto a certain proportion of the total credit, for the intermediaries politics-economic gains, for a few relieving from the responsibility of the earlier guarantees, for the recipients the payments of the earlier loans. In addition when the projects were not completed in one year the money in terms of subsidies which were supposed to be deposited in the accounts of the recipients and adjusted as repayment, the B.D.O. being of the same social group convinced and provided them in cash after a substantial deduction.Even then only two plants could work. Thereafter these were also abondoned due to lack of necessary infrastructure.

The whole process was completed without the actual knowledge of the recipents and social structure of the village. The interests other than actual success of projects motivated this to happen. Such plants were not the need of the recipents but they were motivated for some other interests as by products of this.

IV Analysis and Conclusions

Facts relating to the social structure of the village alongwith earlier experiences, particularly the political and economic field of rural life provide the setting within which the new processes of banking appeared on the scene particularly for weaker sections. Now the questions raised in the introduction of the paper be attempted. Whether really the weakest section of the community have been benefited ? How social structure interacts with the new institutions ? Whether it digests the gains even when an institution is meant for a particular section ? Or to sum up what are the differential consequences of the measure (institution) reaching the village under the cover of rural development.

In the first instance the bank provided loans to 53 persons, 41 of whom were Harijans those designated as weaker section. That too these 41 are from the 29 families as in 10 cases loans were granted to two members and in one to three members of the same family, whereas there are some 150 households of Harijans thus leaving 80% untouched or to say one in five households has been benefitted. In the second instance of biogas also loans were granted to the persons of these families. These ten families provide a case of concentration of or at least a multiplicity of beneficiaries among the Harijans. It is further borne out that they are concentrated in the two kin groups inhabiting the same neighbourhood. In occupational terms among the 41 earlier recipients and more than half (9) of new, 20 have plots of land for agriculture and also for residence provided by the Village Land Managing Committee under state policies of distribution of Panchayat land to landless during the last decade (before the loans). The second section represented by a substantial number 16 having other occupations like shoe making, milk cattle, sewing, cycle repair etc. The weakest section constitute only of the 5 families who neither have land nor any other occupation just labour in the first instance and they left at all in the second instance of financing. This suggests the selectivity of the process in favour of the more well to do among the Harijans designated as weaker sections leaving 80% among them whereas there are non Harijan lower caste Hindus and Muslims who are equally poor and are in a significant proportion in the village. Only 5 families of such groups have been benefited in the first instance and remained untouched in the second instance. These are only those who have better connections (by service etc.) with the then Pradhan, Ex-Pradhan and other leading persons active in the process. The persons of 10 concentration families are known to have been taking active part in the Socio-political activities, by becoming up-Pradhan, member of the village Panchayat, credit co-operative society of the village etc.

It is a clear that receiving the benefits meant for the weaker sections of society is differentially distributed with persons controlling the main approaches of other benefits too.

The interaction of the social structure is seen in terms of providing intermediaries between the bank and the recipients. The crucial guarantee in the first instance were provided in two thirds of the cases by the higher caste elite group (who provided in a number of cases 3 to 14 each). Among the Harijans only 16 that too leading persons from the concentration families, provided 32 guarantees. In 41 Harijans only seven had both the guarantors from their own group. In 18 cases one Harijan and one higher caste, in 16 both higher caste. Among the Harijan guarantors except 4 all were recipients. Thus the nature of closed network is apparant that some selected families among the Scheduled Castes have been able to play this role, and they are also the beneficiaries.

Eight persons were in light frequently—the Village School Head Master a Tyagi, the then Prandhan Jain and his eldest son, the present Pradhan Rohella Pathan, an Ex-Pradhan a Tyagi, the then up-Pradhan a Kasai, a Brahmin and a Tyagi who is landless but available for liason work, he has been benefited in the second instance as a weaker section. These persons are important units of the social structure who entered in the process at crucial stages. had their interests—political support and association of services with beneficiaries a competition among them as a need of political support. They conceived their role indispensible and prestigious when some body comes from outside and asks for help. In the second instance though the formal role as guarantors was eliminated but the persons remained important, were also serving their own economic interests particularly in case of Jain Pradhan is son as intermediary, moneylender, manufacturer and supplier, liason between the agencies and underhand dealings. In these cases it was clear that for obtaining various certificates from Tehsil and banks the intermediaries made money.

To sum up as is clear in the first instances only a section among the weaker sections has been benefited. This beneficiary section is largely not the poorest section among them. On the second occasion the beneficiaries are more or less the same group. They were having earlier experiences of participation in the socio-political activities, benefited by other measures earlier too. The strong and prestigious units of the two divisions for political support, prestige and other for snatching economic gains came in the process. Some Scheduled Caste persons also from the concentration families better off than others in their social group got used to the new institutions, again largely making use of the benefits. On the second occasion the elite higher castes group also upto large extent replaced by their own persons. Thus it shows that among the Scheduled Castes self sufficiency is coming in terms of leadership for negotiating their own issues state policy gains. As was clear in the first instance a competitive polity accelerated the support for Harijans—the verticular division of the upper strata in the competition increased interaction with Scheduled Castes and resulting into the growing problem solving leadership among them.

The consequences as intended on the part of the bank officials completing the targets and the bank as a commercial organization partly resulting into selectivity of the stronger section of the weaker sections ensuring repayment and fulfilling their targets too. Partly the complexity of the process greased by economic gains. The development agency the Block Development Officials on the one hand completing targets and on the other involving monetary gains. The persons combining various roles together are benefited. The people are learning the ethoes of negotiating various agencies which together provide such benefits. Thus consequences are differentially distributed for officials of various agencies, the village elite, new up coming problem solvers within the Scheduled Castes and non-Scheduled Castes. All of them have different socio-political and economic interests. This sum of interests resulting the benefits of state meant for weaker sections in favour of the selected better part of the designated weaker section Scheduled Castes and the benefits are just limited the large part which is actually weaker is left out. Thus suggesting the stronger the units of social structure more gains are likely to flow in its favour.

References

1. Chauhan, B.R. 1967 : *A Rajasthan Village*, Delhi.
2. Merton, R.K.1968 : *Social Theory and Social Structure*, New Delhi, Amerind.
3. Pundir, J.K. 1980 : *Law and Weaker Sections*, in I.N. Tiwary (ed.), *Challenges and Alternatives*, Meerut, U.P. Pol. Sc. Asso.
4. Srinivas, M.N. 1976 : *The Remembered Village*, New Delhi, Oxford.

FOURTEEN

Social Profiles of Scheduled Castes in Perspective of Development Programmes : A Case Study of Koraon Block

(Allahabad District)

Dr. R.S. Pandey

Introduction

In the post-independence period and parlicularly after initiation of planning, various measures have been undertaken to improve the economic and social conditions of Scheduled Castes and Tribal population all over the country. The Government has taken many development programmes, but the programmes have not succeeded in making the desired impact which should have been preceptible in terms of life, development of human resources and distributive justice. Although the development process in itself was supported to creat more earning opportunities to such sections of the society. Extensive educational facilities and reservation in jobs for Scheduled Castes and Tribes was also aimed to hasten their betterment. The present study aims to analyse the impact of development upon social conditions of Scheduled Castes of ten selected villages in Koran Block of Allahabad District, which has the highest percentage of Scheduled Castes population. Both primary and secondary data has made use for the study. Purposive stratified sampling was used for selecting ten villages out of 193 villages of the Block, one from each nyaya panchayat, varying in caste and size composition. Total study compiises of 866 respondent households having a total population of 6404.

The Study Area

The study area Koraon Block is one of the four Blocks of Meja Tahsil, which is one of the 8 Tahsils of Allahabad District (U.P). It lies between 24° 48′ M to 25° 10′ N Lat. and 81° 45′ E to 82° 14′ E Long. and commands an area of 63,742.67 hectare. It sustains a population of 1,32,337 (1981) giving a population density of 207 persons per km and stand first in the Scheduled Castss population amongst the four Blocks of Meja Tahsil, which is nearly 29.81 (39,448) percent of the total population of the Block (1981). The study region Koraon Block is extreme southern part of Yamunapar tract. This region is entirely different from the rest of the District Allahabad. It geographically belongs to Bundelkhand or Mirzapur. Almost the surface of the ground of Koraon Block is broken by small hills and rocky outcrops but in the north of the Belan river there is fairly rich plain of alluvium. The region enjoys typical monsoon climate with seasonal variation in rainfal (85.6 mm annually) and temperature (winter 15° C and Summer 35° C). On the whole its geographical setting provides a base for its agricultural economy which is the source of livelihood for nearly 93% of its total population. Industrially it is a backward area and also lacks an efficient transport network as nearly 36% of its geographical area is inaccessible because of difficult terrain.

Social Structure

The Scheduled Castes of the Koraon Block, are socially less privileged as the vested interests of privileged upper castes work against their legitimate interests. Broadly speaking, social development of the Scheduled Castes has been hampered because of their educational backwardness, social alienation, poverty and economic deprivation. In most of the sample villages, there is a remarkable social alienation among themselves because of purity-pollution relationships. The Chamars do not accept water or food from the Dhobhis, the Doms; the Dhobis do not wash the clothes of other Scheduled Castes and are more attuned to the traditional Jajmani system. They have no socio-ritual relationship to each other.

It has been observed that the elite-mass gap is much wider than that among the general population and consequently their susceptibility to social hierarchy is more pronounced. The common denominator of the Scheduled Castes often ignores this social reality which reflects multiplicity of their sub-division which are arrayed one against another and often resort to the same disguised practices of untouchability and discrimination which is accorded to them by the higher castes.

The impact of development programmes on social development of the Scheduled Castes is to be examined in the light of these social realities which often work as limiting factors. Education is the catalyst of development and is measured in terms of literacy levels. Next come health and housing conditions which are basic ingredients of social improvement for improving living conditions and quality of life of Scheduled Castes.

Literacy Levels

The Government has taken many steps for removal of mass illiteracy and ignorance among the Scheduled Castes, because literacy is a measure of socio-economic development and political consciousness of social group. However, the social inputs designed for improvement in their literacy levels have been by and large wasted without desired result.

Table 1 shows the comparative position of literacy levels of total population and Scheduled Castes population in Uttar Pradesh, Allahabad District and study region.

It clearly shows that Koraon Block has a much lower literacy rate for the Scheduled Castes, than that of the State and District. The study region is almost rural area, therefore the literacy has been calculated for rural literacy. The total literacy of the Koraon Block is 18.51 per cent (males 31.55 per cent and females 4.14 per cent) whereas the Scheduled Castes literacy is 6.28 per cent (males 11.90 per cent and females 0.57 per cent).

The literacy patterns of the Sample Scheduled Castes population of Koraon Block, have been analysed in the Table 2. The abstract given at the end of Table 2, shows that 8.37 per cent of the total sample population was literate (males 14.61 per cent and females 1.36 per cent) in 1988. A comparison of these literacy rates with the literacy rates given in 1981 census for the Scheduled Castes in rural area of the Koraon Block, surely indicates a perceptible change because of the various educational facilities provided by the Government. Table 2 also gives the literacy structure according to age-groups. The age-group 15-44 carries the highest literacy (Total 13.02 percent : males 23.85 per cent and females 1.58 per cent) followed by the age-group of 5-14 which has total literacy rate of 7.34 per cent (boys 12.23 and girls 2.09 per cent). The age group of 15-44 has been also benefitted by the adult education programmes. But it indicates that the female response to both formal and non-formal education is very meagre. The female education in 5-14 age-group (2.39 per cent as compared to the total females literates of 1.36 per cent) shows a heatening position because if

TABLE 1

Literacy Pattern in U.P., Allahabad District and Koraon Block (in Per Cent 1981)

S. No.	*Region*	*Population Group*	*Persons*	*Male*	*Female*
1.	Uttar Pradesh	Total	27.40	38.90	14.42
		Rural	23.34	35.40	9.86
		Urban	45.91	54.44	35.82
2.	Allahabad District	Total	27.99	41.51	12.81
		Rural	21.02	35.28	5.53
		Urban	55.24	64.76	43.66
3.	Allahabad District S. C. Literacy	Total	12.11	20.59	2.91
		Rural	9.30	17.20	0.80
		Urban	32.06	43.75	18.49
4.	Koraon Block's Total Literacy	Total	18.51	31.55	4.14
5.	Koraon Block's S. C. Literacy	Total	6.28	11.90	0.57

Source : Census of India 1981, Part II—B

TABLE 2

Literacy Patterns of Sample Scheduled Castes Population in Koraon Block

Koraon Block	*Age — Groups*														
Literacy Level	*5 to 14*			*15 to 44*			*45 to 59*			*60+*			*Total Literate*		
	P	*M*	*F*	*P*	*M*	*F*	*P*	*M*	*F*	*P*	*M*	*F*	*P*	*M*	*F*
1	2	3	4	5	6	7	8	9	10	11	12	13	14	15	16
1. Primary	72	58	14	92	84	8	18	16	2	9	9	—	191	167	24
2. Middle	47	43	4	108	101	7	15	15	—	3	3	—	173	162	11
3. High School/ Intermediate	19	18	1	102	97	5	14	14	—	—	—	—	135	129	6
4. Graduate	—	—	—	23	23	—	—	—	—	—	—	—	23	23	—
5. Trained	—	—	—	14	14	—	—	—	—	—	—	—	14	14	—
6. Diploma	—	—	—	—	—	—	—	—	—	—	—	—	—	—	—
Total Lilterates	138	119	19	339	319	20	47	45	2	12	12	—	536	495	41

1	2	3	4	5	6	7	8	9	10	11	12	13	14	15	16
Total Population	1878	973	905	2602	1337	1265	774	430	344	352	195	157	6404	3388	3016
Total Literates as percentage to Total Population	7.34	12.23	2.09	13.02	23.85	1.58	6.07	10.46	0.58	3.40	6.15	—	8.37	14.61	1.36

the female literacy goes up the overall literacy will improve as the females constitute nearly 50 per cent of the total population.

Table 3 gives age and sex-wise levels of literacy. In the age-group of 5-14 years 52.17 per cent literates have primary school level, 34.06 per cent of them have the middle school level and hardly 13.77 per cent of literates could claim high school education. The proportion of the females in this education level is almost negligible because of their later entry and heavier drop-outs.

The age-group of 15-44 has representatives in all educational levels, but their high percentage in primary stage establishes that the Scheduled Castes children go for schooling at a much later stage. Their falling rate in Middle, High School/Intermediate/Graduate and Training levels of literacy presents their drop-out trend which is more spectacular in the case of females Scheduled Castes, who lose their share much faster than males. The age-groups of 45-59 and 60 + show that formerly educational levels of the Scheduled Castes were much lower but they have appreciably improved because of the increasing educational facilities provided by the Government during the successive Five Year Plans.

On the basis of foregoing discussion it may be hypothesised that the level of literacy varies directly with female literacy and the impact of urbanisation, Its policy implication is that unless the mass literacy of the Scheduled Castes population and more specifically of their females is increased, the educational levels will not rise as envisaged in the educational planning programmes. For the Scheduled Castes the school going age corresponds with the working age and their child labour, is common both, directly and in disguised form as their traditional occupations and poverty stand to their way and force them to become bread earners by direct participation in labour force or by doing odd jobs of fuel collection, tending cattle or baby

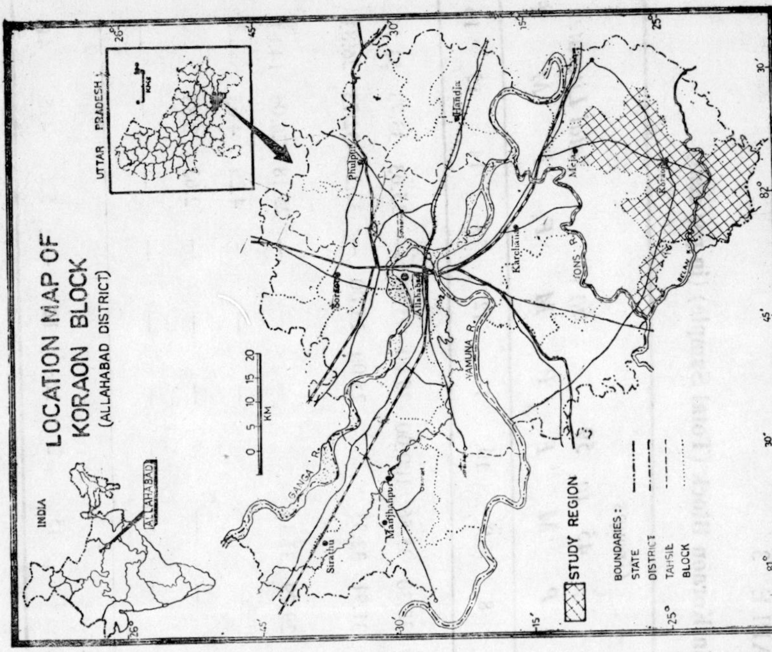
LOCATION MAP OF
KORAON BLOCK
(ALLAHABAD DISTRICT)
INDIA
ALLAHABAD
UTTAR PRADESH
0 5 10 15 20
KM
GANGA R.
YAMUNA R.
TONS R.
BELAN R.
Sirathu
Manjhanpur
Soraon
Phulpur
Handia
Allahabad
Karchana
Meja
Koraon
STUDY REGION
BOUNDARIES :
STATE
DISTRICT
TAHSIL
BLOCK

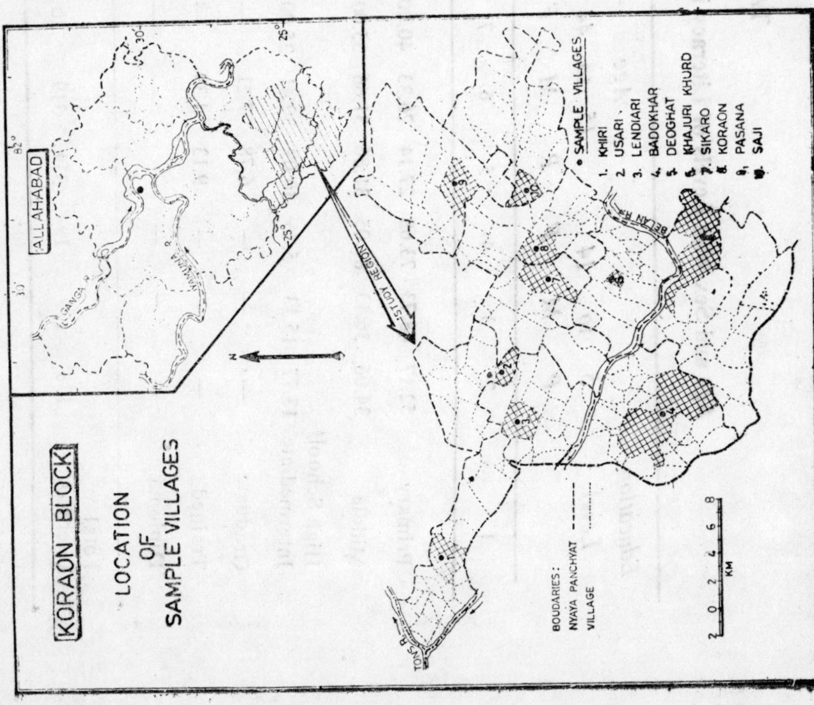
KORAON BLOCK
LOCATION
OF
SAMPLE VILLAGES
ALLAHABAD
GANGA
YAMUNA R
STUDY REGION
N
• SAMPLE VILLAGES
1. KHIRI
2. USARI
3. LENDIARI
4. BADOKHAR
5. DEOGHAT
6. KHAJURI KHURD
7. SIKARO
8. KORAON
9. PASANA
10. SAJI
BOUDARIES:
NYAYA PANCHYAT
VILLAGE
0 2 4 6 8
KM
TONS R.
BELAN R.

TABLE 3

Age and Sex-wise Levels of Literacy in Koraon Block (Total Sample) (in per cent)

Education Level	*Age — Groups* 5 to 14			15 to 44			45 to 59			60+			*Total Literates*		
	P	*M*	*F*	*P*	*M*	*F*	*P*	*M*	*F*	*P*	*M*	*F*	*P*	*M*	*F*
1	2	3	4	5	6	7	8	9	10	11	12	13	14	15	16
Primary	52.17	48.73	73.68	27.14	26.33	40.00	38.30	35.56	100.00	75.00	75.00	—	35.63	33.73	53.54
Middle	34.06	36.13	81.05	31.86	31.66	35.00	31.91	33.33		25 00	25.00	—	32.27	32.73	26.83
High School/ Intermediate	13.77	15.13	5.26	30.09	30.41	25.00	29.79	31.11		—	—	—	25.18	26.06	14.63
Graduate	—	—	—	6.78	7.21	—	—	—		—	—	—	4.29	4.65	—
Trained	—	—	—	9.13	4.39	—	—	—		—	—	—	2.63	2.83	—
Diploma	—	—	—	—	—	—	—	—	—	—	—	—	—	—	—
Total Literates	138	119	19	339	319	20	47	45	2	12	12	—	536	495	41

1	2	3	4	5	6	7	8	9	10	11	12	13	14	15	16
Total Literates as Percetage to Total Population	7.34	12.23	2.09	13.02	23.85	1.58	6.07	10.46	0.58	3.40	6.15	—	8.37	14.61	1.36
Total Population	1878	973	905	2602	1337	1265	774	430	344	352	195	157	6404	3388	3016

sitting. That is why fewer Scheduled Castes children are studying in schools as compared to those belonging to the general population and the position is certainly the worst for the Scheduled Castes.

Table 4 analyses the trend of schooling of the Scheduled Castes children in Koraon Block. It vividly reveals the pattern of drop-outs and the declining share of the Scheduled Castes children as they move from primary (classes 1 to 5) to middle (Classes 6 to 8) to High School/Intermediate/Degree Classes. The Scheduled Caste girls (1983-84) fare much worse than the Scheduled Caste boys in this vertical movement in literacy levels : the respective figures for boys and girls are 25.95 and 20.49 (Primary stage), 15.38 and 13.10 (Middle School Stage), 13.67 and 8.60 (High School/Intermediate Stage) and 20.99 and 13.40 (Degree Stage).

In 1981-82 the percentage of Scheduled Castes girls in total girls enrolment was barely 16.72 per cent which rose to 20.49 per cent in 1983-84 in the Primary classes. In higher levels of literacy the change was more encouraging. Certainly it is a welcome change and bears an unmistakable impact of the educational facilities provided to the Scheduled Caste children by the Government. But these data must be accepted with caution because they are the result of target approach which is basically quantitative and leaves much scope for qualitative improvement. The enquiries reveal that the Scheduled Castes have not shared equitably the benefits of massive adult education programmes which has not clicked so far. In total reckoning these economically deprived castes remain at a lower level for educational achievement.

Housing Conditions

Their housing conditions remain hopelessly poor and consequently, adversely affect their health and living conditions. My survey shows that the vast majority of houses owned by the

TABLE 4

Trend of Schooling of Scheduled Caste Children in Koraon Block

Year	*Classes 1 to 5*		*Classes 6 to 8*		*Classes 9 to 12*		*Degree Classes*	
	Scheduled Castes Students As Percentage to Total Students							
	Boys	*Girls*	*Boys*	*Girls*	*Boys*	*Girls*	*Boys*	*Girls*
1980-81 (Total)	25.99	16.72	17.95	8.89	12.59	4.04	N.A.	N.A.
1982-83 (Total)	26.72	19.46	15.84	10.83	12.77	4.41	12.74	3.33
1983-84 (Total)	25.95	20.49	15.38	13.10	13.67	8.60	20.99	13.40

Source : Statistical Bulltetin, Allahabad District.

Scheduled Castes lack in essential physical and social requirements of a shelter. They are often overcrowded, structurally unsound, dingy, infested with vermin and lacking in facilities for cooking and stooring food and often devoid of drinking water facilities.

Table 5 gives a peep into their living accommodation. 31.76 per cent of the sample households have a single-roomed accommodation which meets all their requirements of a sleeping sitting, kitchen, store and domesticated animals. Only 23.33 per cent households have separate rooms for sleeping and sitting purposes whereas 3.35 per cent of households have separate rooms for sitting purposes only. 19.16 per cent households have separate kitchen and only 16.52 per cent of them have separate cattle-sheds (vide Table 6). This analysis gives a very gloomy picture of the living accommodation of the Scheduled Castes households in the study region. 34.06 per cent of the sample Scheduled Castes households have double-roomed accommodation whereas 18.71 per cent households have tripple-roomed accommodation and 15.47 per cent well to do households, have four or more rooms in their houses (vide table 5).

Table 7 gives the structural conditions of the sample Scheduled Caste households on village basis. It shows that 87.30 per cent of sample Scheduled Caste households live in thatched houses with mud walls whereas harely 6.12 per cent of the houses are made of tiled roofs with mud walls and hardly 1.50 per cent houses are pucca ones. Of course, there are variations from village to village. Two out of ten sample villages have not a single pucca house which is the symbol of economic well being and social status. Tiled roofs with mud walls are found in all sample villages and tin roofs with brick walls occur in barely 0.23 per cent houses which are found in two villages. The thatched roofs with bamboo walls account 3.00 per cent of households but their proportion varies from village to village.

TABLE 5

Accommodation in Sample Villages of Karaon Block

Sample Village	Number of Households							Total No. of Households
	One Roomed	Two Roomed	Three Roomed	Four Roomed	Five Roomed	Six Roomed	Seven Roomed	
1	2	3	4	5	6	7	8	9
Khiri	39	36	17	5	3	1	2	103
Usari	6	4	5	3	1	—	—	19
Lendiari	17	29	30	18	6	3	1	104
Badokhar	36	57	18	7	2	1	—	121
Deoghat	21	27	15	8	4	2	—	77
Khajuri Khurd	7	11	6	5	3	—	—	32
Sikaro	24	19	14	11	6	2	—	76

(Contd)

(Continued from Previous Table)

1	2	3	4	5	6	7	8	9
Koraon	60	38	18	8	2	1	1	128
Pasana	38	43	21	9	3	2	1	117
Semari-Baghrai	27	31	18	7	5	1	—	89
Total	275	295	162	81	35	13	5	866
Percentage	31.76	34.06	18.71	9.35	4.04	1.50	0.58	100.00

TABLE 6

Usages of Rooms in Sample Villages

Sample	*Kitchen*	*Sleeping*	*Sleeping and Sitting*	*Sitting only*	*All Use*	*Animals only*	*Total House holds*
1. Khiri	20	11	25	4	29	14	103
2. Usari	4	2	5	1	5	2	19
3. Lendiari	21	10	27	3	31	12	104
4. Badokhar	24	13	28	5	34	17	121
5. Deoghat	16	8	18	3	22	10	77
6. Khajuri-Khurd	6	3	7	1	9	6	32
7. Sikaro	15	7	17	2	21	14	76
8. Koraon	23	12	29	3	35	26	128
9. Pasana	21	10	26	4	32	24	117
10. Semari-Baghrai	16	8	20	3	24	18	89
Total	166	84	202	29	242	143	866
Percentage	19.16	9.70	23.33	3 35	27.94	16.52	100 00

TABLE 7

Housing Conditions in the Sample Villages

Sample Villages	*Total No. of Households*	*Tin Roof with Brick Wall*	*Tin Roof with Mud Wall*	*Tin Roof with Bamboo Wall*	*Tiled Roof with Brick Walls*
1	2	3	4	5	6
1. Khiri	103	—	—	—	1
2. Usari	19	—	—	—	—
3. Lendiari	104	—	—	—	2
4. Badokhar	121	1	—	—	2
5. Deoghat	77	—	—	—	1
6. Khajuri Khurd	32	—	—	—	—
7. Sikaro	76	—	—	—	—
8. Koraon	128	1	1	—	2
9. Pasana	117	—	—	—	1
10. Semari-Baghrai	89	—	—	—	—
Total	866	2	1	—	9
Percentage		0.23	0.12	—	1.03

Tiled Roof with Bamboo Walls	Tiled Roof with Mud Walls	Thatched Roof with Mud Walls	Thatched Roof with Bamboo Walls	Pucca Houses	Type of Floor Mud or Dung	Brick-laid	Cement Plaster
7	8	9	10	11	12	13	14
1	6	90	3	2	102	—	1
—	2	17	2	—	19	—	—
1	7	92	3	1	102	2	—
1	9	104	4	3	118	2	1
—	6	67	3	1	76	1	—
—	3	28	2	—	31	1	—
1	5	65	3	1	75	1	—
2	8	111	2	3	125	1	2
—	4	104	2	1	116	—	1
—	3	78	2	1	88	1	—
6	53	756	26	13	852	9	5
0.69	6.12	87.30	3.00	1.50	98.38	1.04	0.59

The building material used in floor construction is a more critical measure of economic conditions and living styles. In my sample households as many as 98.38 per cent houses have mud floors; some with a plaster of cowdung. Hardly 1.04 per cent houses have floors made of brick, whereas 0.59 per cent are plastered with cement, even though the Government have provided them bricks and cement on subsidized rates. Vary few Scheduled Castes housenolds have opted for the subsidized houses built for the weaker sections as they neither suit their purpose nor pocket. Often their sites are unattractive. On the whole it can be stated that mud and dung floors are predominant. All the pucca houses with concrete roofs, tin roofs and tiled roofs do not share the credit of having pucca, that means brick laid and cement plastered floors.

The sources of drinking water available to the Scheduled Castes households in the Sample Villages have been analysed in the Table—8. The tap water is available to 6.81 per cent of the Sample Scheduled Castes households and 12.59 per cent of them have been provided with handpumps, but the remaining households (88.02 per cent) still depend upon wells. In the many of the sample villages except few households, who have a handpump facility, many of them depend on open wells for drinking water.

In few Sample Villages each of them has hardly one or two hand pumps. As the drinking water facilities are limited, public wells are crowded and quarrels are not uncommon for getting water supplies.

In the study region the water level of the lowlands and the plains is fairly high ranging from 20 to 35 feet below the surface; but the sub-soil is frequently unstable and unprotected well cannot be made. In the hilly country of the south the water level is very deep and the construction of wells is very difficult and costly if not impossible. In many parts there is great scarcity of water, even the drinking purposes and often the available supply is of a very inferior quality.

TABLE 8

Sources of Drinking Water Available to the Sample Scheduled Caste Households

Sl. No.	Sample Villages	No. of Households	Sources of Drinking Water: Taps	Hand Pumps	Open Walls	Pond	Others	Refuse Disposal: Dumping Outside	Dumping in pits	Compositing	Burning	Others	Water Disposal: Soak Pit	Open Drains/Letout in open Space
1	2	3	4	5	6	7	8	9	10	11	12	13	14	15
1.	Khiri	103	8	12	83	—	—	12	87	2	—	2	—	103
2.	Usari	19	—	3	16	—	—	2	16	1	—	—	—	19
3.	Lendiari	104	—	11	93	—	—	11	85	5	—	3	—	104
4.	Badokhar	121	12	17	89	—	3	18	97	3	—	3	1	120
5.	Deoghat	77	18	9	48	—	2	9	65	1	—	2	—	77
6.	Khajuri-Khurd	32	—	3	29	—	—	2	28	—	—	2	—	32
7.	Sikaro	76	—	12	64	—	—	13	60	2	—	1	—	76
8.	Koraon	128	21	20	87	—	—	21	101	4	—	2	2	126

(Contd.)

(*Continued from Previous Table*)

1	2	3	4	5	6	7	8	9	10	11	12	13	14	15
9.	Pasana	117	—	14	103	—	—	16	96	2	—	3	—	117
10.	Semari-Baghrai	89	—	8	81	—	—	12	74	2	—	1	—	89
Total		866	59	109	693	—	5	116	704	22	—	19	3	863
Percentage			6·81	12.59	80.02	—	0.58	13.09	81.87	2.54	—	2.19	3 35	99.65

The refuse disposal methods of the Scheduled Castes also add to the insanitary conditions in their neighbourhoods. As a common practice they make use of nearby open spaces or fields for lavatory purposes. Our survey shows that as many as 13.09 of their households dump refuse just outside their houses, only 81.87 per cent of them use dumping pits a little away from the residential neighbourhood. However, the households which are engaged in agriculture and rear livestock, nearly 2.54 per cent of them make use of cowdung and other refuse for compost. As there is scarcity of fuel wood, most of the households use dung cakes for cooking their meals and waste cowdung, which is a valuable organic manure.

My sample survey reveals that the insanitary conditions of the Scheduled Castes househoulds are made worse by their methods of water disposal. As many as 99.65 per cent of households just let refuse water flow in open space in the court-yards and streets. Hardly 0.35 per cent have soak pits. Only three sample households had soak pits out of 866 sample house-holds. The problem of health and sanitation is aggravated due to lack of drainage facilities. Most of the houses have kuchha open drains overflowing with human excreta, refuse and dirty water.

Health Conditions

The study region is generally considered healthy. My survey also reveals that the health conditions of the sample Scheduled Castes population are far from being satisfactory. My enquiries show stark conditions of under-nutrition and malnutrition because of their poverty, low living standard and ignorance. Many workers who are engaged in physical labour hardly get an intake of 1700-2000 calories per day, when their requirements are of 2500—calories. The protein, vitamin and mineral require-ments of a balanced diet are not available even to 19.5 per cent of the Sample Scheduled Castes households. They suffer mostly from deficiency diseases, as their habits of cleanliness are bad and their residential houses are in insanitary conditions. Their mortality and morbidity rates are also high. The infectious diseases like cholera, small pox/measels have more than usual tolls. The incidence of tuberculosis, penumonia, bronchitis, dysentary, hook worm and round worm is high. As their houses are small and dingy the epedemics prove disastrous because of adverse environmental conditions and contamination of food and water. In the canal irrigated and water logged areas the incidence of malaria has particularly increased.

Among other diseases the most common are bowel complaints, pulmonary ailments and affections of the skin, eyes and ears. Mention should also be made of the peculiar form of the lacomotor paralysis which is very prevalent in the study region. It is undoubtedly due to the consumption of the small pea which is extensively grown in those areas. This paralysis appcars to bc pcrmanent and is not curcd by thc discontinuance of the use of the grain, which affects animals as well as human beings. The sufferers naturally belong to the poorer class of cultivators.

My survey reveals that hardly 44.69 per cent (vide Table—9) of the Sample Scheduled Castes households ever availed of the medical and health services provided by the Government. It appears that they have not een properly motivated for use of health and medical facilities provided by the Government. Their ignorance, illiteracy and superstitions come in their way and discourage them.

The Integrated Child and Women Development Service Project was launched in 1975-76. It is certainly a well conceived plan for takin the health and nutritional problems of the children and women of weaker sections of the society, particularly the Scheduled Castes and Scheduled Tribes. However, my Sample survey reveals that hardly 4.27 per cent Scheduled Castes households have been benefitted by aforesaid programme. Six out of ten Sample Villages are still not covered by the programme. The impact of the programme is noticeable in the

TABLE 9

Medical and Health Facilities and Impact of ICWDSP in Sample Villages

Sl. No.	Sample Villages	*Medcial and Health Facilities Availed*		*Impact of ICWDSP in Sample Villages*	
		Total No. of Households	*No. of Beneficiary Households*	*S. C. Households covered under Integrated Children & Women Development Programme & Anganwadis*	*No. of S.C. Beneficiries*
1.	Khiri	103	48	4	22
2.	Usari	19	8	—	—
3,	Lendiari	104	51	6	29
4.	Badokhar	121	56	4	21
5.	Deoghat	77	35	2	9
6.	Khajuri Khurd	32	10	—	—
7.	Sikaro	76	31	3	16
8.	Koraon	128	62	8	38
9.	Pasana	117	47	6	27
10.	Semari-Baghrai	89	39	4	18
Total		866	387	37	180
Percentage			44.69	4.27	2.81

villages which lies in the close vicinity of the Block Headquarter. During my field survey I have noted that the Scheduled Caste children and women do not get equitable share among the beneficiaries selected under the programme. Now it is very necessary to bring out the coordination in the policy and implementation of various programmes relating to health and nutrition, and to create awareness about improving the food habits amongst the rural masses. Nutrition education is the best way by which the route of under the malnutrition can be changed, and this education must relate with their local environment and food availability as well as their respective traditions.

References

Alexander, K.C. : "*Economic Development and Social Change*, 1982, Journal of Rural Development, Vol. I, No. 6, p.p. 864-913.

Barnabas, A.P. & Mehta, S. : *Caste in Changing India*, 1963, (New Delhi, Indian Institute of Public Administration.)

Beteille, A. : *Social Inequality*, 1969, (Penguin Book Series).

Blunt, E.A.H. : *The Caste System of Northern India*, 1969, (Delhi, S. Chand and Co.)

Census of India : *Census of India*, 1971, Uttar Pradesh, Part II-C, (II), Social and Cultural Tables.

Census of India : *District Census Hand Book*, 1971, Allahabad Part-XIII A, B and C.

Census of India : *Census of India*, 1981, Uttar Pradesh Part II B, Primary Census Abstract.

Kamble, N.D. : *The Scheduled Castes*, 1982, (Ashish Publishing House, New Delhi).

Malik, S. : *Social Integration of Scheduled Castes*, 1979 (New Delhi, Abhinav Publishers)

Mukherjee, A.B. : *The Chamars of U.P.*, A Study of Social Geography. (New Delhi, Inter-India Publication).

Nevil, H.R. : *Allahabad District Gazetteer*, 1928.

Singh, L.R. : *Impact of Development Programmes on Socio-Economic Conditions of Scheduled Castes in Rae Bareli District*, U.P., (Research Project), 1986.

Srinivas, M.N. : *Future of Indian Caste*, 1979, E & P.W., Annual Number, Vol. XIV, Nos. 7 & 8, pp. 237-254.

FIFTEEN

Self Fulfilling Prophesy: An Insight into Perjudice Vs Reality

Prof. R. Venkataratnam

The Constitution of India in its Articles 29 and 30 declares to provide equality of opportunity to all in education, liberty and justice. However the same Constitution provides protection to certain classes of people who need special encouragement and help to reach that "Equality" the Constitution attempts to guarentee. It is a well known dictum that there can be no equality among unequals.

The affirmative action or the so called protective discrimination given in order to protect equality is under constant threat from vested interests. Whenever the question of renewal of this protection comes there is vociferous oppasition to it. Paradoxically the groups that enjoy some degree of such protection do also resent affirmative action taken in favour of the Scheduled Castes and Scheduled Tribes in India.

Tamil Nadu has a fairly long histroy of struggles to protect the interests of the backward and the oppressed sections of the population. The results of the struggles are reflected in the reservations that were quaranteed in the Constitution and the actions taken by the successive Governments. The present Government emerging from that tradition continues the same. These concessions have really helped the descendents of a large number of caste groups in education in employment, and in political power. However it is well known that the benefits of such affirmative action have always gone to the better off sections of the backward groups. To certain extent this is true of Scheduled Castes also. The poorer and the worse off sections have always suffered from the beginning. It is in these midst of this scenerio one can perceive the resentment of the advantaged groups against all reservations and the powerful few of the disadvantaged groups against concessions for Scheduled Castes and Scheduled Tribes. This resentment often leads to hatred and whenever opportunity comes the members of the oppressed group particularly from Scheduled Castes and Scheduled Tribes are discriminated against. This is clearly seen from the representations given to Scheduled Castes and Scheduled Tribes in the faculties of universities in Tamil Nadu.

The situation indicates that only five and less than five per cent of the strength of the faculty is from the Scheduled Castes and Scheduled Tribes. Surprisingly one would find that out of the 12 universities except two professional universities where original recruitment took place through Government quota system there is some representation in the faculty for Scheduled Castes and Scheduled Tribes. Of the remaining non-professional universities in only one rotation system exists which provides some opportunity for the entry of candidate from these groups.

The privileged groups often attribute this phenomenon to the disadvantaged groups indifference to the opportunities provided for learning, and as a consequence to claim for other benefits. Often such critics forget that the condition under which the Scheduled Castes and Scheduled Tribes are placed in the socio-economic environment which is hostile to their progress,

It is often forgotten that low-level incomes of the underprivileged do not encourage their children to go to school for the simple reason that the additional income that the children bring will be lost to the family. In many locations schools will be inaccessible for reasons of physical distance, social seggregation and austricism, as well as pressure from non-Scheduled Caste and non-Scheduled Tribe groups as not to establish schools in Scheduled Caste and Scheduled Tribe areas. In spite of these drawbacks and social discouragement if boys and girls manage to pass out of schools they (some of them atleast) do not have the required economic strength to enter into colleges and later to the universities.

Often people criticise that Scheduled Castes and Scheduled Tribes do not make use of the opportunities provided by the Government in the form of fee concessions and scholarships. Rarely if ever people analyse the quantum of monetary support or help provided by the fee concessions and scholarships.

In our experience we have observed that the quantum of support provided by the state is totally inadequate for a student to live in self respect in an educational system where hierarchy still exists. Let me eloborate this. Let us take the case of a student in a college who hails from a Scheduled Caste or Scheduled Tribe family. Under the existing rules of the Tamil Nadu Government students of backward class with less than Rs. 1500/- as annual income as parental income are eligible for half fee concession. The hostellers will get approximately Rs. 972/- per annum in addition to half fee concession. The students of most backward classes of the same income group will get full fee concession and hostellers from these group will get about Rs. 972/-. Students from Scheduled Caste and Scheduled Tribe get full fee concessions plus Rs. 2400/- per annum for the hostellers. On an average a college or an university works for about 10 months in a year. The hostel dues per month will run approximately Rs, 400/- per month which means hostel fees alone for one year (10 months) will be Rs. 4000/- for a student. Very often we fail to realise that a student can not live in a university campus with food alone. An average student requires the following for minimum expenses.

1.	Pocket money	: Rs. 100/- per month
2.	Washing and toilet shop	: Rs. 20/- per month
3.	Books	: Rs. 50/- per month
4.	Travelling	: Rs. 10/- per month
	Total	Rs. 180/- per month
	For ten months : 180 × 10	Rs. 1800/- per year
5.	Clothes	Rs. 1000/- per year
	Total expenses	Rs. 2800/- per year

The hostel expenses plus other expenses cited above make a total of Rs. 6800/- per year for a college or a university student to continue as a student. However the scholarships provide only Rs. 2400/- that is less than 50 per cent of the total cost required.

The advantaged groups assume that all the participants from Scheduled Caste and Scheduled Tribe groups in the college or university learning process have the capacity to meet the balance cost. This is an erroneous position as most of our Scheduled Caste and Scheduled Tribe brethern live below the poverty line and cannot afford this expensive education. Naturally members of Scheduled Caste and Scheduled Tribe groups cannot think of higher education in this situation. Therefore the reservation percentages with the quota system, the communal rotation and so on become meaningless. To say that Scheduled Castes and Scheduled Tribes do not make use of facilities and opportunities is like victim blaming and a self-fulfilling prophesy. You victimise the Scheduled Castes and Scheduled Tribes by making him unequal in economic and social terms and complain that they do not attempt to use the privileges.

The traditionally privileged groups do not want the Schedule Castes and Scheduled Tribes to be literated; to be well educated; to be in good position of employment and occupy positions of power. The reservations and the quantum of support given to make use of the reservations are so inadequate that the Scheduled Caste and Scheduled Tribe groups do not fulfil the expectations of the privileged. This is the self fulfilling prophesy of the privileged and the exploitative sections of the society.